1983

Linking Philosophy and Practice

Sharan B. Merriam, *Editor*

NEW DIRECTIONS FOR CONTINUING EDUCATION

ALAN B. KNOX, *Editor-in-Chief*

Number 15, September 1982

Paperback sourcebooks in
The Jossey-Bass Higher Education Series

Jossey-Bass Inc., Publishers
San Francisco • Washington • London

Linking Philosophy and Practice
Number 15, September 1982
      Sharan B. Merriam, *Editor*

New Directions for Continuing Education Series
Alan B. Knox, *Editor-in-Chief*

New Directions for Continuing Education (publication number
USPS 493-930) is published quarterly by Jossey-Bass Inc.,
Publishers. Second-class postage rates paid at San Francisco,
California, and at additional mailing offices.

Correspondence:
Subscriptions, single-issue orders, change of address notices,
undelivered copies, and other correspondence should be sent to
New Directions Subscriptions, Jossey-Bass Inc., Publishers,
433 California Street, San Francisco, California 94104.

Editorial correspondence should be sent to the Editor-in-Chief,
Alan B. Knox, Teacher Education Building, Room 264,
University of Wisconsin, 225 North Mills Street, Madison,
Wisconsin 53706.

Library of Congress Catalogue Card Number LC 81-48476
International Standard Serial Number ISSN 0195-2242
International Standard Book Number ISBN 87589-889-0

Cover art by Willi Baum
Manufactured in the United States of America

Ordering Information

The paperback sourcebooks listed below are published quarterly and can be ordered either by subscription or as single copies.

Subscriptions cost $35.00 per year for institutions, agencies, and libraries. Individuals can subscribe at the special rate of $21.00 per year *if payment is by personal check.* (Note that the full rate of $35.00 applies if payment is by institutional check, even if the subscription is designated for an individual.) Standing orders are accepted.

Single copies are available at $7.95 when payment accompanies order, and *all single-copy orders under $25.00 must include payment.* (California, Washington, D.C., New Jersey, and New York residents please include appropriate sales tax.) For billed orders, cost per copy is $7.95 plus postage and handling. (Prices subject to change without notice.)

To ensure correct and prompt delivery, all orders must give either the *name of an individual* or an *official purchase order number.* Please submit your order as follows:

Subscriptions: specify series and subscription year.
Single Copies: specify sourcebook code and issue number (such as, CE8).

Mail orders for United States and Possessions, Latin America, Canada, Japan, Australia, and New Zealand to:
    Jossey-Bass Inc., Publishers
    433 California Street
    San Francisco, California 94104

Mail orders for all other parts of the world to:
    Jossey-Bass Limited
    28 Banner Street
    London EC1Y 8QE

New Directions for Continuing Education Series
Alan B. Knox, *Editor-in-Chief*

CE1 *Enhancing Proficiencies of Continuing Educators,* Alan B. Knox
CE2 *Programming for Adults Facing Mid-Life Change,* Alan B. Knox
CE3 *Assessing the Impact of Continuing Education,* Alan B. Knox
CE4 *Attracting Able Instructors of Adults,* M. Alan Brown, Harlan G. Copeland
CE5 *Providing Continuing Education by Media and Technology,* Martin N. Chamberlain
CE6 *Teaching Adults Effectively,* Alan B. Knox
CE7 *Assessing Educational Needs of Adults,* Floyd C. Pennington
CE8 *Reaching Hard-to-Reach Adults,* Gordon G. Darkenwald, Gordon A. Larson
CE9 *Strengthening Internal Support for Continuing Education,* James C. Votruba
CE10 *Advising and Counseling Adult Learners,* Frank R. DiSilvestro

Contents

Editor's Notes

Administrators, counselors, and teachers who work with adults are concerned with both the process and product of educational practice. There are many resources available for the practitioner who seeks concrete information on program planning, needs assessments, instructional strategies, and so on. Likewise, several authors have written on the general goals of continuing education and the philosophical assumptions underlying the field. The purpose of this sourcebook is to consider practice and philosophy together and to explore the relationship between the two as it manifests itself in adult and continuing education.

In Chapter One, John Elias sketches the history of philosophy's relationship to practice and then suggests that the preferable way of understanding the connection is to study it as a tension-bearing relationship characterized by explanation, criticism, direction, and imagination. His chapter thus provides a framework for the case examples which follow.

Chapters Two, Three, and Four center on some of the underlying issues involved in the task of planning programs. Don Campbell thoughtfully analyzes the effect mandatory continuing education requirements have had on program planning in the medical profession. Bill Koeper writes about the weighting of various criteria and the juggling of organizational and personal goals in determining which courses are offered in the training division of an insurance company. In Chapter Four, Merrill Ewert discusses four problems encountered by educators who attempt to involve learners in program planning.

Philosophical biases, whether or not they are articulated, enter into the decision-making process in adult and continuing education practice. Chapter Five offers a glimpse into what goes on behind everyday decisions in the allocation of resources in a continuing education division of a large urban community college. Chapter Six is a contrast in setting, but some of the same issues in decision making emerge. Carolyn Farrell discusses the development of a continuing education program at a small college in Iowa.

Evaluation presents an interesting dilemma for continuing educators. Practitioners are committed to encouraging growth in a supportive atmosphere but at the same time must ensure that learning has occurred or that a program has accomplished its objectives. Jones and Lowe discuss this dilemma with respect to the evaluation of adult basic education teachers.

The assessment of prior learning is but one of several issues that bring theory and practice into conflict in nontraditional forms of continuing education. Phyllis Cunningham offers an insightful analysis of the interaction of philosophy and practice in her discussion of the three forms of nontraditional education.

The seven case examples in Chapters Two through Eight provide the basis for a summary analysis presented in Chapter Nine. In this chapter, the interaction of theory and practice with reference to the case examples is reviewed and suggestions are made for how practitioners can help strengthen the bond between theory and practice.

For those who have thought about the role of theory in practice, this sourcebook offers examples from a wide variety of settings as well as raises issues involved in translating philosophy into action. For others who are new to the field of continuing education, this volume provides a beginning point for the examination of one's own values and offers support for developing a personal philosophical framework.

Sharan B. Merriam
Editor

Sharan B. Merriam is associate professor of adult and
continuing education at Northern Illinois University.
She is coauthor of Philosophical Foundations of Adult Education
and Adult Education: Foundations of Practice.

The relationship between philosophy and practice
can be characterized as explanatory, critical,
directive, and imaginative.

The Theory-Practice Split

John L. Elias

It is the nature of philosophical problems that they are never answered to the
satisfaction of everyone, in part because these problems touch upon the basic
tensions and polarities of human existence. Thus, philosophers of every age
have offered explanations of freedom and determinism, individual and societal
rights, good and evil, and truth and falsehood. The great works in philosophy
are those that deal with these and similar problems in ways that are found per-
suasive for persons beyond the writer's generation.

One of the most difficult problems that philosophers address is the relationship between philosophy and action, or between theory and practice. At
the heart of this problem is the tension between knowing and doing — between
knowing the truth and doing the truth, between knowing the good and doing
the good. For many philosophers, this problem is best expressed as the tension
between theoretical wisdom and practical wisdom, or, more simply, as the relationship between theory (or philosophy) and practice. The purpose of this
chapter is to examine the relationship between theory and practice.

Opposition Between Theory and Practice:
Superiority of Theory

Greek philosophers grappled with the issue of theory and practice primarily in an attempt to determine which kind of knowledge was more worthwhile. The classical position in Greek philosophy is found in the writings of
Aristotle. A common interpretation of his thought is that theory and practice

S. Merriam (Ed.). *New Directions for Continuing Education: Linking Philosophy and Practice*, no. 15.
San Francisco: Jossey-Bass, September 1982.

are in opposition, but Aristotle's position contains more subtle variations than this common interpretation allows.

Aristotle (McKeon, 1941) described three types of human life and activity: *theoria, praxis,* and *poesis.* *Theoria* (theory) was the speculative life in which one searched for truth solely by a contemplative and reflective process. To theorize was to achieve wisdom by understanding the most basic principles of life. The achievement of theoretical wisdom was the most complete form of happiness. Aristotle called the practical life *praxis* and described it as reflective engagement in some area of society. Praxis included two moments: action and reflection. To practice, for Aristotle, was to achieve practical wisdom, for example, in such areas as business, politics, and education. *Poesis* was Aristotle's term for the productive life. It entailed the making of artifacts or concrete things. Through it a person developed a craft, a skill, or an art.

Despite Aristotle's careful distinctions, his legacy to medieval philosophy included a number of exaggerated dualisms, including the opposition between theory and practice and the superiority of theory over practice. Medieval philosophy continued and reinforced this tradition. Theory, which was the activity of the speculative or contemplative life, was highly valued because it gave true knowledge. The practical life afforded experiences from which only opinions could be formed. What one learned from experience was considered of little value when compared with what one learned from a contemplation of first principles or the First Principle, God.

This position led to the notion that, in knowing and acting, it is always best to go from theory to practice. It devalued common experience and practice as sources of true knowledge. It exaggerated the value of theory and speculation in human life. It led to a depreciation and suspicion of manual work and practical involvement. In some cultures, this viewpoint led to rigid class distinctions that were devised according to what types of activities people engaged in.

In education, this viewpoint has had a certain number of well-known, harmful effects. It has led to the belief that certain subjects (philosophy, mathematics, literature, and history) are in themselves more valuable than are others (natural sciences, vocational education, technological education, and career education). For many years this viewpoint prevented the introduction of subjects of a practical nature into the curriculum. The struggle between progressive education and liberal education in this country has been largely centered on the issue of the relative importance of the theoretical and the practical.

Theory and Practice in Opposition: The Superiority of Practice

In the middle of the seventeenth century, Francis Bacon, the British philosopher of science, introduced a new mode of thought to the Western world. Bacon argued that the surest way to knowledge was through an examination of facts gained from experience. This empirical or experiential mode of knowing was a principal element in the philosophy of pragmatism, a powerful influence in American social and educational thought.

The pragmatic spirit is responsible for the bias toward the practical and useful that characterizes American life and American education. A basic premise of pragmatism is that we determine what is good or true by examining practical consequences. Ideas are good and true to the extent that they help individuals to understand their experiences and solve problems, and lead to satisfying results. The emphasis on the practical is seen in the pragmatist's deep concern with reforming social institutions. Action is what is most necessary in this endeavor.

The educational implications of the pragmatic viewpoint are seen in educational theories that arose in opposition to classical and liberal education. These theories depended less on earlier accepted theories than on direct experience and observation. More attention was placed on methods and people in the educational process. The process of learning was analyzed in an empirical manner. A science of teaching developed that was founded on a study of particular methodologies. The education of teachers became primarily training in practical skills rather than an education in classical educational theories.

While Aristotle is associated with the view that theory is superior to practice, one of John Dewey's legacies (1916) to education has been the idea that practice is superior to theory. In other words, Dewey does not maintain a distinction between the two. Since Dewey's time, the field of education has been baised toward the practical. Courses in administration and methodology greatly outnumber courses in philosophy and policy studies. Research studies that deal with practical aspects of education are much more common than theoretical or philosophical studies.

The fact that the academic field of adult and continuing education arose during the height of the progressive period of American educational history helps to explain the strongly pragmatic nature of this field. Until recently, little systematic attention has been given to the theoretical foundations of continuing education. The major works in the field have been books on program planning and teaching methodologies. Most papers given at research conferences have dealt with practical rather than theoretical issues. Those who pursue continuing education in this country and those who study in the field are most often motivated by practical purposes.

Theory and Practice: A Dialectical Relationship

A preferable way of understanding the relationship between theory and practice is to view it as a dialectical relationship. Hegel (1953) made one of the first moves in this direction when he rejected the separation of theory from practice and emphasized the unity between the two. He attempted to maintain the productive tension between practical life experience and the theories derived from the experiences of previous generations.

Hegel's analysis of practice was criticized by Marx (1976) for being overly idealistic and unduly contemplative. He argued that the dialectic between theory and practice was resolved by Hegel into a unity in which only theory dominated. Marx preferred a more materialistic and historical praxis. His approach to theory and practice came from his analysis of the relationships among work, capital, and structures of society. For Marx, theory represented the consciousness that arises from practical involvement. Once a theory has evolved, it must inform further practice; thus, a dialectical unity is posited between the two.

A weakness in Marx's approach to theory and practice is the limited way in which he defined praxis and, consequently, theory. By restricting his view of praxis to work, property relationships, and revolutionary action, he advocated economic determinism and, therefore, a deterministic view of the relationship between theory and practice. Domination by a capitalistic system determines a consciousness or theory of reality (broadly described as alienation) that necessarily leads to a revolutionary praxis. However one thinks of capitalist systems, it is clear that living in them does not necessitate a sense of domination, oppression, and alienation. It is also clear that people arrive at different theories or types of consciousness even though they are involved in the same praxis. Thus, the human mind adds more to theory than Marx appears to have allowed.

Some of the weaknesses in Marx's theory are corrected by Jügen Habermas (1973), a contemporary German philosopher of social theory. Habermas, in dialogue with Marxists, has placed more emphasis on theory as the critical reflection on self and society. He points out that particular interests, attitudes, and ideologies can influence theories. In developing his theory for the relationship of theory to praxis, Habermas adds a broader range of human activities (science, art, religion, history, psychology, and political activity) to work and property relations.

The conception of theory as critical reflection on practice has received its strongest educational development in the works of Paulo Freire (1970, 1973). Freire advocates a dialogic approach to education with his theory of conscientization. The purpose of education is to bring people to a critical awareness of the social realities in which they are immersed. Critical awareness entails the denunciation of oppressive reality and the prophetic announcement of a utopian reality that is free of oppression. To conscientize others is to aid them in decoding reality, "stripping it down so as to get to know the myths that deceive and perpetuate the dominating structure" (1974, p. 27). This conscientization is made possible through praxis—reflection and action on the world with the intent to transform it.

In viewing the relationship between theory and practice as a dialectic or tension between the two, an effort must be made to maintain the integrity of both theory and practice and not to allow one to attain superiority over the other.

The Dialectic Between Theory and Practice in Education

Education is rightly termed a practice in human life. As such, it can be likened to law, medicine, business, and sports. A practice is "any form of activity specified by a system of rules, which defines offices, roles, moves, defenses, and so on, and which gives the activity its structure" (Rawls, 1971, p. 55). The attempt to understand rationally the various aspects of a practice is called philosophy or theory; thus, we have a philosophy or theory of medicine, law, and education. The question to be considered is what are the characteristics of the relationship that exists between philosophy or theory and practice. At least four elements appear to be present in this relationship: explanation, criticism, direction, and imagination.

Explanation. A philosophy or a theory explains a practice. Educational theories attempt to explain the ends and objectives of the practice of education. They help to decide which activities are appropriately considered educational activities. Theory attempts to do in a systematic way what common sense does in an unorganized manner. Theory attempts to probe goals, relationships, methods, structures, institutions, norms and procedures of evaluation.

Practice, however, helps us understand theories. Just as we learn about love by experiencing love, we learn about education by experiencing education either as a teacher or as a learner. One can begin by theorizing or practicing. But practice impels thoughtful persons to a deeper examination of theories, especially since there is rarely a one-to-one correspondence between theory and practice. Practice often supplies the concrete examples needed to give insight into a theory. It is often the case that practice comes before theory and gives rise to theory, according to the axiom "theory begins after sundown."

Criticism. Theories "criticize" practice. They test the practice of education according to accepted rational criteria. Theories of instruction, learning, and evaluation question why these activities are organized in the way they are. Educational theories subject well-known educational practices to criticism. What is the underlying rationale of the Great Books program, and is it a defensible one? Can a market approach to continuing education programming be defended on rational grounds? What are the assumptions behind such behavioristic practices as behavioral modification, programmed instruction, and competency-based teacher education? This critical function of theory recommends it to educational practitioners. It is essential that persons who use particular methods recognize the underlying assumptions of those methods and approaches.

Practice has great potential in offering constructive criticism to theories. Practice may show that theories are inadequate for explaining reality. By putting a theory into practice, one often sees ways that the theory should be modified. It is the failure of a theory to meet the test of practice that often leads to the abandonment of that theory. When people resist learning in encounter groups, simulation situations, and games, some modifications in these theories are called for. The resistance of many people to programmed forms of instruction may indicate certain theoretical weaknesses in the theory underlying this practice.

Direction. Educational theories, like all other theories of practice, have the important function of directing action. Whoever theorizes in education should not have the elaboration of theory in mind as the end product, but rather the development of guidelines for practice. The general goals of educational practice are well known: the formation of character, the cultivation of intelligence, the promotion of knowledge, education for work and leisure, and education for citizenship and social change. Educational theory is organized along lines that direct practice activities: teaching, training, learning, evaluation, or administration. Because of this directive character, theories of practice, such as education, differ from scientific theories whose functions are to describe, explain, control and predict. This distinction must be recognized if one is to avoid underestimating the importance of theories for practice.

Educational practice is also directive. It gives direction to both theorists and researchers. Practice directs theorists to facts, phenomena, and events that must be explained and criticized; it reveals the incongruities that are not accounted for in the prevailing theories. Freire's (1970, 1973) experience in literacy education with peasants in northeast Brazil directed him away from a static view of education and toward a dynamic view of education as the development of critical political consciousness. Carl Rogers' (1969) experience with patients directed him away from a behavioristic understanding of the person and toward a humanistic perspective in which freedom, relationship, and authenticity are highly valued.

Imagination. Thus far, the relationship between theory and practice has been viewed purely from a rational perspective. To complete this discussion, one must look at theory and practice from the perspective of the imagination. At times, theories "imagine" or "construct" possible practices. Though theory most often arises from attempts to explain, criticize, and direct practice, in some cases it begins with a denial of present practice and with attempts to imagine new and different practices. Theory is often utopian in its rejection of present practices and in its call for new and radical forms of practice. The theorizing of Plato in *The Republic* (1945), of Thomas More in *Utopia* (1955), and B. F. Skinner in *Walden II* (1948) are examples of such imaginative theorizing. In the early 1970s, Paul Goodman and Ivan Illich imagined a society in which formal schooling was greatly reduced and informal modes of education predominated. The debate over their proposals helped clarify educational theory and practice.

As theory imagines practice, so does practice often present concrete situations that serve to stretch the imagination of theorists. Dewey's theory of progressive education derived as much from his experience with extraordinary educational practices (described in *Schools of Tomorrow,* 1962) as it did from his intellectual immersion in the educational theories of Rousseau, Pestalozzi, and Hegel. Myles Horton's (Adams and Horton, 1975) radical theory of adult education arose from his imaginative educational efforts in dealing with social problems in the South. Imagination is often found in the person of action who develops a concrete solution to a particular problem, creates a unique educational experiment, or fashions a new type of relationship with learners.

Toward Healing the Split Between Theory and Practice

Thus far the theory-practice problem has been discussed chiefly as a theoretical issue. This problem also exists at a practical level. In education, there is a social division between theoreticians or researchers and practitioners. Theoreticians and researchers are usually found at universities or foundations, while the practitioners work in other settings. When these two groups do come together, it is usually the theoreticians and researchers who speak and the practitioners who listen. Theoreticians usually write for and read *Adult Education* and other scholarly journals; practitioners usually write for and read *Lifelong Learning*. While some degree of social separation is necessary for professional identity and growth, one can still question the degree to which this separation contributes to the crisis between theory and practice in the field of education.

Increased efforts should be made to close the gap between these two groups. Healing this gap will also help resolve some of the problems of the theory-practice split. This sourcebook explores ways in which philosophy of the theoreticians and researchers can be linked to the actions of the practitioners.

Graduate Schools. Professors of adult and continuing education should continually examine their teaching to see whether or not it is consistent with sound principles of continuing education. It is also important for professors occasionally to engage in teaching adults outside the unversity setting. People who are involved in teaching in such practical fields as medicine, business, education, politics, and counseling need direct practice to enhance and enrich their teaching.

A social split often exists in graduate schools of education between theoreticians and empirical researchers. Those who teach theoretical foundations of education are often isolated from those involved in empirically-based disciplines. Through a creative use of teaching, conferences, and collaborative scholarly research efforts, this social split may be healed. Collaboration between theoreticians and empirical researchers is necessary if research in continuing education is to become theoretically sophisticated. Empirical research in the field of continuing education sorely needs attention to theory development and theory testing.

Conferences. The number of conferences in the field of adult and continuing education increases annually. There are two types of conferences or meetings. In the professional conference, theoreticians (usually a rather small number) and empirical researchers deliver papers and reports of research findings or methods. In the other type of conference, the theoreticians and researchers attempt to apply their theories to practice for an audience of practitioners. Both types of conferences are organized by academics for their own professional purposes. A structure is needed in which practitioners talk to academics and academics seriously listen. Only by listening to practitioners will academics be able to work out the practical implications of their theories and research and thus ensure not only that their theories and research are applied in practice but also that they are really worth applying.

Journals. The theory-practice split is most manifest in the journals and magazines in adult and continuing education. Academics publish in and read professional journals. Their academic life and progress depend upon their involvement with these journals. Academics who publish in less scholarly publications are viewed with suspicion. Practitioners rarely read the scholarly journals and usually confine their reading to more practically oriented publications. The merits of this practice are questionable. On occasion both types of publications should open their pages to articles emanating from the other side. Creative editors might find ways to explore the same problem from both theoretical and practical vantage points. Collaborative writing between theoreticians and practitioners might be encouraged.

The healing of the split between theory or philosophy and practice is an urgent issue. The issue goes beyond the theory-practice split in graduate schools, conferences, and journals. At issue is the very nature of the profession of education. Because education is by its very nature a practice, the profession of education must develop both sound theories and sound practices, and it must constantly work for the integration of these at both theoretical and practical levels. This chapter has provided some thoughts on achieving this needed integration. In our theorizing and in our actions, we need to maintain the dialectical tension of theory and practice. This can be done if we recognize that both theory and practice have powers of explanation, criticism, direction, and imagination. The integrity of both must be maintained in their integration. In education, theory without practice can become irrelevant and practice without theory can become mindless.

References

Adams, F., and Horton, M. *Unearthing Seeds of Fire: The Idea of Highlander.* Winston-Salem, N.C.: John F. Blair, 1975.

Bacon, F. *The Works of Francis Bacon.* London: Longman and Co., 1876–1890.

Dewey, J. *Democracy and Education.* New York: Macmillan, 1916.

Dewey, J., and Dewey, E. *Schools of Tomorrow.* New York: Dutton, 1962. (Originally published 1916.)

Freire, P. *Pedagogy of the Oppressed.* New York: Seabury, 1970.

Freire, P. *Education for Critical Consciousness.* New York: Seabury, 1973.

Freire, P. "Conscientization." *Cross Currents,* 1974, *24* (1), 23–81.

Goodman, P. *The New Reformation.* New York: Random House, 1970.

Habermas, J. *Theory and Practice.* Boston: Beacon, 1973.

Hegel, G. W. F. *Reason in History: A General Introduction to the Philosophy of History.* New York: Liberal Arts Press, 1953.

Illich, I. *Deschooling Society.* New York: Harper & Row, 1970.

McKeon, R. (Ed.). *The Basic Works of Aristotle.* New York: Random House, 1941.

Marx, K. "The Critique of Hegelian Philosophy." In P. Connerton (Ed.), *Critical Sociology.* New York: Penguin, 1976.

More, T. "Utopia." In F. R. White (Ed.), *Famous Utopias of the Renaissance.* New York: Macmillan, 1955.

Plato. *The Republic.* (Trans. F. Cornford). New York: Oxford, 1945.

Rawls, J. *A Theory of Justice.* Cambridge, Mass.: Harvard University Press, 1971.

Rogers, C. *Freedom to Learn.* Columbus, Ohio: Merrill, 1969.

Skinner, B. F. *Walden Two.* New York: Macmillan, 1948.

John L. Elias is associate professor of adult education and director of the Program in Adult Religious Education in Fordham University's Graduate School of Religion and Religious Education. He is the author of Foundations and Practice of Adult Religious Education *(Krieger, 1982) and coauthor of* Philosophical Foundations of Adult Education *(Krieger, 1980).*

*Mandatory continuing education may have improved the quality
of educational activities in some ways, but it has inhibited the
quality in other ways.*

Mandatory Continuing
Professional Education:
Help or Hindrance to
Quality Education?

M. Donald Campbell

Mandatory continuing education has become a reality for a number of professions in the past decade. The health professions especially have been affected.
Although the rate at which states are implementing mandatory continuing
professional education requirements may be decreasing, many states still require continuing education for a variety of professions (Watkins, 1980). A few
states have rescinded mandatory continuing education legislation for a particular profession, but for many professional groups, such legislation is still in
force.

As mandatory continuing professional education has proliferated, a
number of essays have been published that discuss its pros and cons from
various philosophical perspectives. Recent examples include Mattran (1981),
Rockhill (1981), Smith (1981), and Ohliger (1981). This chapter will not offer
yet another philosophical perspective on mandatory continuing education. Instead, it will describe some of the ways mandatory continuing education has
influenced program planning activity from the perspective of one practitioner.
This practitioner directs a university-based office of continuing medical edu-

S. Merriam (Ed.). *New Directions for Continuing Education: Linking Philosophy and Practice*, no. 15.
San Francisco: Jossey-Bass, September 1982.

cation in Illinois. Although he has administrative responsibility for continuing education programs conducted for nurses, pharmacists, dentists, and other health professionals, all examples discussed in the chapter are drawn from continuing medical education activity. (The reader should know that this practitioner is also the author of this chapter.)

In Illinois, physicians must accumulate a total of 100 hours of continuing education activity every two years in order to maintain their licenses to practice medicine in the state. At the end of this two-year period, they report the hours they have spent in such activity when they renew their licenses. In addition to this quantity of hours, quality of the educational experiences is also of concern to the state. One reason for requiring physicians to continue their education is to improve medical care. If continuing medical education activity results in high quality medical care, one can conclude that high quality educational activity should occur.

An important question, then, is whether high quality continuing medical education occurs in an environment in which it is required. This question is too complex to be answered in this chapter. But another interesting question is whether mandatory continuing education has influenced the quality of continuing education activities in which physicians participate. In what ways has it improved the quality of these activities? In what ways has it inhibited the quality of them?

Positive Influences of Mandatory Continuing Medical Education

Three ways mandatory continuing medical education may have improved the quality of continuing education activities should be noted: enhancing the value of informal educational activities, accrediting providers of formally organized continuing medical education programs, and encouraging a systematic planning process.

Mandatory continuing education requirements can enhance the value of relatively informal educational opportunities and self-directed learning activities. This may seem surprising, because sitting through a series of formally organized classes is a pervasive image of mandatory education. Yet of the 100 hours of continuing medical education activity that physicians must accumulate within a two-year period, only twenty hours must be earned by participating in formally organized continuing education programs. Up to eighty hours can be earned in less formal ways. Examples include teaching medical students or residents, participation on hospital committees that review the quality of health care provided in the hospital, and a variety of self-study programs.

Participation in these less formal learning activities per se does not guarantee a high quality educational experience. Yet good reasons can be advanced for considering these three examples as high quality educational experiences. Teaching a subject is often considered the best way to learn it, so a physician who presents a seminar to medical students or residents will probably gain a high quality learning experience from organizing the material to be taught, especially when this seminar is scrutinized by an accredited medical school. Committees that review the quality of health care in a local hospital focus on problems immediately relevant to practitioners. Physicians who serve on these committees cannot help but gain new insights on the best ways to solve these problems. In addition, physicians who engage in self-study activities select topics they most want to understand or master. If they complete these programs and earn a given number of continuing education hours, one can assume they have learned much about these topics. Although empirical evidence has not been presented to show that these examples are high quality educational experiences, physicians who participate in them probably learn more than they would by sitting through a series of formally-organized lectures on a given topic.

Two other ways that mandatory continuing medical education may have improved the quality of educational activities involve formally organized continuing education programs. These ways entail accrediting providers of continuing medical education programs and encouraging a systematic planning process. Rather than trying to monitor the quality of all continuing education programs offered, the state attempts to ensure program quality by blessing certain continuing education providers accreditation status. Essentially, two kinds of providers are recognized as offering programs which satisfy the state's requirements. Some hospitals are accredited through the state medical society as providers; medical schools are also recognized as providers through a nationally administered accreditation process. Thus, if an accredited provider offers a continuing medical education program, the state assures itself and others that the program is a high quality education experience. Non-accredited institutions may ensure the quality of programs they offer by obtaining cosponsorship from an accredited provider.

Once organizations are accredited as providers, they must then ensure the quality of programs they sponsor. Using a systematic program planning process is an attempt to do this. Evaluating these programs is another way to monitor program quality. Other ways of ensuring high quality are employed during various planning stages, such as establishing the need for a particular program, specifying the audience, developing behavioral objectives, selecting appropriate content to meet these objectives, identifying qualified resource persons to conduct sessions, and basing decisions on previous program evaluations whenever possible. Instead of quickly contacting an entertaining speaker to lecture on a topic of interest to the program planners, attempts are made to find out what physicians in various specialties need to know, what a particular program can realistically accomplish, what learning activities would be most effective, and how to report the program's value.

For each program conducted, providers maintain a permanent file containing a description of the planning process, summaries of content discussed, and evaluation data collected, plus a list of all physicians participating in the program. The program files are important sources of information each time the accrediting body reviews the hospital's or medical school's continuing medical education effort. Showing the accreditors that a systematic planning process has been used is one way these organizations maintain their status as approved providers of continuing medical education.

Negative Influences of Mandatory Continuing Medical Education

Three potentially positive influences of mandatory continuing medical education on the quality of educational activity have been mentioned: enhancing the value of relatively informal educational activities, accrediting providers of formally organized continuing medical education programs, and encouraging a systematic planning process. Ironically, these very same factors can also exert negative influences on the quality of educational experiences.

Informal Educational Activities. Although physicians in Illinois can earn up to 80 percent of their required hours through informal educational opportunities and self-directed learning activities, the number of formally organized programs seems to be increasing. Hospital medical staffs may conduct several regular activities which clearly qualify as informal educational opportunities, but strong interest is often expressed in having them recognized as formal education programs. For example, two different hospitals recently requested cosponsorship for their respective tumor conferences from the medical school with which this writer is affiliated. Physicians participating in these conferences could easily report their hours spent, using the appropriate category of informal educational activity. Such reporting would not require cosponsorship by an accredited continuing medical education provider. But perhaps desiring prestige and legitimacy, both hospitals wanted their tumor conferences approved as formally organized programs.

Associated with a desire for formally organized programs is frequent reliance on traditional teaching methods in these programs. Lectures followed by questions from the audience are used very extensively. Less traditional learning activities, such as case study analyses, problem-solving activities, simulations, and other "hands-on" activities, tend to be overlooked. The main innovation in continuing medical education has been the use of carefully prepared 35 millimeter slides, deftly presented with a carousel projector and electronic pointer. The use of slides during a medical lecture is almost as common as a chalkboard in a mathematics classroom. Just as math professors may mask their insecurity by turning their backs to the class, so physicians may mask their insecurity by turning off the lights.

Accreditation of Providers. Although accrediting providers may improve the quality of formally organized programs, access to these programs can be a problem. Do physicians have sufficient opportunity to participate in at least twenty hours of formally organized accredited programs? Or has the accreditation system made such participation unrealistic for some physicians, for example, rural physicians in solo practice? Legislating mandatory continuing medical education is not in itself sufficient; opportunities to participate must also exist, or else the legislation is ineffective.

The best way to ensure sufficient opportunity to participate in formally organized programs is for accredited providers to offer them in local areas. Physicians could travel to other communities or states to attend conferences or short courses lasting as long as two weeks. These offerings, though, are very expensive. In addition to a substantial registration fee and travel expenses, physicians must also consider the cost of time away from their practices. Continuing medical education programs cosponsored by a local provider, on the other hand, are much less expensive. Fees are usually lower, travel expenses are minimal, and time away from medical practice is reduced substantially. These programs can be scheduled to fit more conveniently into the physician's schedule. Often they are planned as a monthly or weekly series of four-hour Saturday morning conferences or noonhour discussions. An additional benefit is that local programs can focus on medical care problems frequently faced in that particular area.

Do enough accredited providers exist to make locally offered programs a reality? The process of becoming an accredited provider of formally organized continuing medical education is time-consuming and expensive. The institution must pay a fee, but more significantly, must maintain a separate budget and staff to administer continuing education. Because hospitals and other health-related organizations are not educational institutions per se, many of these institutions do not seek accreditation. But local programs can be a reality through a cosponsorship arrangement mentioned above. Two or more institutions can jointly plan the program, with the accredited provider responsible for awarding credit and keeping records.

Unfortunately, this cosponsorship approach does not necessarily result in a quality program. A typical example of a jointly sponsored program involves a community hospital working with a nearby medical school. One or more members of the hospital's medical staff develop ideas for a program and begin planning. During the planning process, one of the planners will contact the medical school to propose a cosponsorship arrangement for the program. The planning may be finished when this first contact is made. The planners may not be very interested in the medical school's help in planning the program. Their primary interest in cosponsorship may be to obtain approval as a formally organized program.

This situation creates a dilemma for the medical school. As an accredited provider, it must vouch for the quality of programs it cosponsors. One way to assess program quality is to be involved in planning the program. Thus when a community hospital proposes cosponsorship after a program is essentially planned, the medical school may have a difficult time vouching for its quality. The medical school can refuse to cosponsor programs it has not helped to plan. But the school often does not want to discourage a community hospital from planning continuing medical education programs; as an educational institution, it is generally interested in improving the quality of medical care in the area. More specifically, its students may receive part of their clinical experience in that hospital. Obviously, the school wants physicians supervising its students to continue to learn. To avoid this conflict, the medical school's continuing medical education staff can make periodic contact with community hospitals to discuss ideas for programs and insist on involvement in the early planning stages.

Limited resources, however, make this approach difficult to implement. To participate actively in planning a program might require traveling to the hospital for a planning meeting. If the hospital is located an hour's drive away, such a planning meeting could cost at least one-half day of staff time, plus traveling expenses. Revenue generated from the resulting program may not cover even the travel expenses. Furthermore, the medical school's staff may be working with several hospitals on several different programs at one time. It may also be working on various programs for which the medical school is assuming primary planning responsibility. The medical school, then, may simply be unable to participate actively in planning a cosponsored program, regardless of how early it is contacted.

This means that accrediting providers does not necessarily result in quality education experiences. To enable practicing physicians to satisfy mandatory education requirements, these accredited providers are encouraged to cosponsor formally organized continuing medical education programs with other institutions. Limited resources, however, make influencing the quality of these programs difficult at best.

Systematic Planning Process. Encouraging a systematic approach to program planning does not necessarily result in high quality education either. One problem concerns the planners. Some physicians involved in developing programs do not consider a systematic planning approach valuable. A second problem concerns the planning approach itself. The particular method most widely used has limitations which are not always understood.

Physicians involved in developing programs must document a systematic approach to planning, but in reality they may not have used it. Whether a program is cosponsored by a community hospital and a medical school or is sponsored solely by a medical school, the developer typically submits a program proposal to the school's continuing medical education office for review. The critical parts of this proposal are descriptions of the need for the program, audience to be served, program objectives, learning activities, resource persons, and an evaluation plan. The proposal helps document program quality during reviews of the medical school's status as an accredited provider of formally organized programs.

The proposal, however, may not necessarily be the result of systematic planning. Instead, it may be the program developer's attempt to present a rationale for the program after it is planned. For instance, the program developer may simply present the best statement possible about the need for the program, regardless of whether this need influenced the planning of the program. The physician may view completion of the proposal as a necessary bureaucratic hurdle to negotiate to obtain approval as a formally organized continuing education program. If the program is approved, this success may confirm previous suspicions that educational planning is more a hindrance than a help. The physician may become cynical and view formally organized continuing medical education as insignificant and trivial efforts to accumulate hours toward relicensing.

The medical school's continuing medical education staff can attempt to work with program developers to demonstrate the value of educational planning. Resource limitations, however, again may prevent extensive involvement. Many programs are short one-to-four-hour events. Spending extensive effort on such a short program, even if resources are available, may not be cost-effective. Not all planning meetings will involve a half-day trip to a nearby community, but the number of programs being planned may preclude adequate attention to all of them.

Before casting physicians as villains in a program planning melodrama, the planning approach itself should be examined. The components of this approach mentioned above rely heavily on Tyler's (1949) principles of curriculum planning. Determining needs, developing objectives and learning activities, plus evaluating the program directly match three of his four principles. The remaining principle, organizing resources for learning, is implicit in such tasks as recruiting resource persons, securing adequate facilities, and promoting the program.

Some physicians and administrators of continuing medical education offices may consider the Tyler approach to be the only way to develop continuing education activities. Other approaches to program development may not be considered.

These physicians and administrators may not appreciate some of the philosophical issues involved in program planning. They may be ignorant of criticisms leveled against the Tyler approach (for example, Kliebard, 1970). More recently, Apps (1979) has criticized Tyler's work from the perspective of its use in continuing education. Apps claims that emphasis on determining learners' needs has led to an emphasis on empirical description of needs. An empirical description of a given state compared with some ideal or improved state, however, does not determine a need. This gap between existing and ideal states does not equal a need. Someone must make a value judgment about the situation by saying the gap does in fact mean a need. Apps also notes that Tyler's principles suggest a step-by-step approach to program planning. This emphasis can lead to treating educational planning as a series of steps to accomplish, rather than as a more holistic process.

The danger of a step-by-step approach is that the individual components may be emphasized in isolation from the planning process. Sometimes needs assessments become ends in themselves. The identified needs may not be transformed into a continuing medical education program. When a program is planned, a clear relationship does not always exist between the needs identified and the objectives developed. Nor can the learning activities always accomplish the objectives.

In fairness to Tyler, some criticism of his principles is more the result of how others use them than of what he actually said. For instance, Tyler may not have intended principles to be treated as a series of steps to accomplish in the same order all the time. Instead, he summarized the important elements of curriculum planning. Nor did he intend the individual principles to be employed in isolation from one another. If planners adopt needs assessments as ends in themselves or ignore these needs when developing objectives, that is not Tyler's fault.

These limitations, then, both in the planning approach itself and in the way it is used, can have a negative influence on program quality. The Tyler approach lends itself to a step-by-step view of program planning and places too much emphasis on empirical determination of needs. Physicians developing continuing medical education programs may only pay lip service to a systematic planning approach or may use it in a superficial, distorted way. A medical school's continuing education staff may not have the resources to ensure the planning approach is used correctly.

Thus, although mandatory continuing education may have had some positive influence on the quality of continuing medical education activity, it also has had significant negative influence. To some extent, mandatory continuing education has enhanced the value of relatively informal educational opportunities and self-directed learning activities. These less formal activities can often be more effective than formally organized lectures as educational experiences. The quality of continuing medical education has also been improved by accrediting program providers and by encouraging a systematic planning process. These very factors, however, have also inhibited the quality of educational experiences. Although relatively informal learning activities can satisfy relicensure requirements in Illinois, formally organized programs using traditional teaching methods are perceived as more prestigious and legitimate. Accrediting providers of continuing medical education programs does not necessarily improve the quality of programs. Cosponsorship of programs by accredited providers with other institutions makes quality difficult to monitor. Finally, use of a systematic planning approach does not necessarily result in improved quality, due to limitations both in the Tyler planning approach and in the way it is used.

Implications for the Educator

What does a mandatory continuing medical education environment mean, then, for the educator? Clearly, an educator directing continuing medical education programs must manage a complicated delivery system. Program proposals must be developed and reviewed, relicensure requirements must be interpreted and applied, and participation records must be created, distributed, and filed. In addition, the routine tasks of program delivery (developing and distributing brochures, contracting for facilities, and ensuring that refreshments are available) must be performed. With limited resources available, these management tasks may lead to an assembly-line production model of continuing medical education programming. Indeed the energetic young educator may feel more like a milkman than a teacher.

The educator, then, can either focus on developing the best delivery system possible, or can seek opportunities to introduce alternative planning approaches. At least three approaches to program planning, in addition to those of Tyler, merit consideration. John Dewey's ideas (1956) form the basis of one approach. Instead of first determining the goals of an educational effort and then planning activities to meet these goals, Dewey reverses the process. He starts with a meaningful activity and then determines the educational goals which can be achieved through it.

In continuing medical education, grand rounds are an excellent illustration of Dewey's philosophy. Physicians first made the rounds to regularly check on the progress of their hospitalized patients. Sometimes several physicians made rounds together, perhaps to discuss the best treatment for particular patients. Later they may have realized that making rounds together was also a chance to teach each other more about the practice of medicine. They also may have realized that younger physicians could accompany them and thereby profit from a rich learning opportunity. These grand rounds, then, became a regular educational event. Other activities might also be exploited for their continuing medical education potential. For instance, informal ongoing discussions between physicians and experts in various specialties might be developed into an organized educational activity.

Apps (1979) discusses two other approaches to program planning which may apply to continuing medical education. One is the liberal education approach. With this approach, program planning is based on what an expert wants to teach (Apps, 1979). Courses are organized around people who have something to say about a particular subject. There is no systematic process of determining needs, developing objectives based on these needs, or selecting learning activities to meet these objectives. At first, the liberal education approach may seem irrelevant to continuing medical education. Interestingly enough, though, it may more accurately reflect the process many program planners use. As noted earlier, some physicians document a systematic planning process to get their programs approved, regardless of whether they actually have used this process. Thus, a liberal education approach may often be a more honest statement of how continuing medical education programs grams are planned.

The other approach Apps (1979) describes is that advocated by Paulo Freire (1973). One aspect of Freire's approach which may apply to continuing medical education is his emphasis on problem posing. Apps (1979, p. 124) points out that "people may not always be able to verbalize their most fundamental problems — that only through a process of consciousness-raising are these subsurface problems brought into the open and discussed." A typical needs assessment, then, lacking this problem posing activity, may yield superficial information or result in programs that do not touch on significant practice problems physicians may have. A second aspect is the relationship between reflection and action. Freire's scheme is to reflect on problems that are identified, determine a course of action, try it, reflect some more, and then try a different course of action if necessary. This sequence differs from the usual approach of conducting a single program without any additional opportunities to discuss the results of a particular course of action. A combination of reflection and action may result in more significant continuing medical education, or in education that has a greater impact on practice.

Of course, the demands of managing a continuing medical education program production line may preclude the use of these alternative planning approaches. And as noted earlier, physicians may be cynical about educational planning and rebuff all attempts by an energetic educator to do more than "deliver milk." With extra effort at the right time, however, even milk can become butter or cream.

References

Apps, J. W. *Problems in Continuing Education.* New York: McGraw-Hill, 1979.

Dewey, J. *The School and Society.* Chicago: University of Chicago Press, 1956.

Freire, P. *Education for Critical Consciousness.* New York: Seabury Press, 1973.

Kliebard, H. M. "The Tyler Rationale." *School Review,* 1970, *78* (2), 259–272.

Mattran, K. J. "Mandatory Education Increases Professional Competence." In B. W. Kreitlow and Associates, *Examining Controversies in Adult Education.* San Francisco: Jossey-Bass, 1981.

Ohliger, J. "Dialogue on Mandatory Continuing Education." *Lifelong Learning: The Adult Years,* 1981, *4* (10), 5–7.

Rockhill, K. "Professional Education Should Not Be Mandatory." In B. W. Kreitlow and Associates, *Examining Controversies in Adult Education.* San Francisco: Jossey-Bass, 1981.

Smith, R. R. "Quality in Continuing Pharmaceutical Education." *Lifelong Learning: The Adult Years,* 1981, *4* (10), 4.

Tyler, R. W. *Basic Principles of Curriculum and Instruction.* Chicago: University of Chicago Press, 1949.

Watkins, B. T., "Move to Require Continuing Education for Professionals Appears to be Stalling." *Chronicle of Higher Education,* November 17, 1980, p. 1.

M. Donald Campbell is director of continuing medical education,
School of Clinical Medicine, University of Illinois at the
Medical Center, Urbana-Champaign and assistant professor of
continuing education, University of Illinois at Urbana-Champaign.
He is grateful to colleagues Anne Colgan, Barbara LeGrand,
Marvin Weinstein, and Harold Paul for contributing to the
development of ideas discussed in this chapter.

*Deciding which curriculum will succeed in an
employee development program involves selecting
programs and activities according to five criteria.*

Corporate Curriculum Decision Making

William K. Koeper

As the manager of the Employee Development Department for the home office
of CUNA Mutual Insurance Group, I am responsible for all educational activities other than sales training. Because we offer a wide group of products,
training needs are very diverse.

Our department serves about 1,200 employees. We regularly offer
educational programs in the following areas: Management and Executive Development, Career Development, Technical Education, Departmental Training, Communications, Insurance Education, Company Orientation, Health
Education, and Industry Education. We offer in-house courses and programs
as well as self-study courses, and we send employees to outside seminars.
Courses are taught by our department staff, by employees we recruit to assist
our staff, and by trainers we hire for particular needs. We offer tuition reimbursement for the continuing education of our employees, and we pay bonuses
for the professional insurance examinations they pass.

As manager, I have full responsibility to decide what is offered, in what
form it is offered, when courses will be offered, who will teach, and how the
budget will be distributed. My responsibilities include assessment of needs,
choice and development of curriculum, and evaluation of results. In addition,
the department is responsible for assessing current educational needs of employees, for preparing employees to handle future positions or changes in their

S. Merriam (Ed.). *New Directions for Continuing Education: Linking Philosophy and Practice,* no. 15.
San Francisco: Jossey-Bass, September 1982.

job responsibilities and for employees' personal development (including career planning and personal goal setting). This chapter explores the methods we use to make such program development decisions and our reasons for making decisions as we do.

Five Criteria for Program Decision Making

In deciding which courses and programs to offer, we use the following as bases for our decisions:

1. Courses and programs must fit into our departmental long-range plan.
2. The need must exist as determined by an assessment.
3. Resources must be available to offer the course.
4. It must be marketable to our employee group.
5. Departmental judgment must support the above bases.

These criteria are given varying weight and priority depending on each situation.

Departmental Long-Range Plan. This is used to provide continuity, to ensure that we are in line with overall company objectives, and to maximize the likelihood that we will complete our plans. The educational plan is based on corporate mission statements. Departmental staff prepare their plan, based on past experience as well as on expectations for the future. Thus, one purpose of the evolving plan is to achieve and maintain consensus on departmental objectives. By making our plans known and visible, we learn whether they will be generally accepted or may cause disagreement. In this way, we can resolve disagreements before problems get out of hand. The plan is valuable also in ensuring that, as changes take place, we will be able to view our current actions and revise them when they have not kept pace with these changes.

Part of this plan is a departmental mission statement that generally describes our role for the next five to ten years. That mission is "to increase productivity through advising and assisting in developing all employees to more fully utilize their potentials to meet both organizational and personal goals." Our departmental goals generally explain how we plan to accomplish this mission:

1. To increase our employees' understanding of our organizations and of how they relate to the organizations we serve throughout the world.
2. To help instill a service attitude within the company and in contacts with those outside our company.
3. To address questions of future human resource needs in order to ensure that the quantity and quality of the human resources needed are available.
4. To counsel and assist all employees in planning their careers.
5. To advise and assist all areas of the group in assessing current and future training and development needs, in meeting those needs, and in measuring results.

6. To evaluate and monitor how development efforts are affected by our hiring process, reward system, appraisal system, and work planning system.

In addition, each year we detail the strategies we will use in accomplishing these goals. They serve as the bases for our educational activities and often result in the development of new programs.

Needs Assessment Methods. This keeps us on track with the desires, needs, and goals of all concerned. To ensure that our departmental needs for budget and the needs of our employees continue to be met, we must be sure that we meet corporate goals such as increased productivity, increased income, and decreased expenses. This means we must be sure that we meet the needs of our organization (such as increasing the skills and abilities of our employees, motivating employees, and preparing employees for promotion) at the same time that we meet the needs of individuals. Rapid changes in the finance and insurance industry mean that needs are rapidly changing. Government regulations are changing, investment vehicles are changing, the facts we use to do business are changing. To keep up with these changes, quick, efficient methods of assessment are needed. In this process, it is essential that we give balanced attention to both organizational and individual needs.

Allocating the Resources. The decision to implement each program requires asking the question, "Is this the best use of our budget and employee time?" Management wants to know who benefits, how many benefit, and if there are any measurable results. We must have answers that will justify our past actions and will ensure that our budget requests for future programs will be given proper priority. When making resource allocation decisions, we make value judgments. Needs assessment procedures identify more educational needs than we can address each year. Needs assessment findings are combined with our familiarity with the company over the years. If a resource allocation decision is likely to be questioned by corporate management, more attention will be given to the rationale and to building consensus, than if the decision is quite straightforward.

Marketability. This is determined by our employees: We offer programs and they choose either to attend or not to attend. Therefore, in order to generate substantial attendance, our programs must be both worthwhile and interesting. They either have to clearly meet employee needs, or we must be able to convince employees and their managers that the programs will meet their needs and help them to more efficiently accomplish their objectives. Thus, by participation or non-participation, employees greatly influence our priorities.

Departmental Judgment. Each Employment Development Department employee has areas of responsibility, and in those areas they have experience, education, and exposure to professional associations, literature, and so on. The knowledge and background of these departmental employees form the basis for an important part of the decision-making process for program development. Because we depend on effective human relations throughout the company, this staff expertise cannot be overlooked. Underlying much of this staff judgment is an effort to balance attention to both individual needs and organizational goals. Attention to company expectations includes making the case that an educational program will benefit the organization. Effective working relationships between departmental staff and company personnel, especially key managers, are essential to achieve and maintain this consensus. Our approach reflects an internal marketing orientation.

Examples of Program Decisions

When we began offering management training, needs assessment was used to decide which topics were needed most. We had no long-range plan, no idea of what would be marketable, and little judgment on which to base decisions because we were a new department. Each manager and executive was asked to rank his or her top preferences from fourteen possible programs. From those preferences we chose four courses to offer: Motivation, Leadership, Time Management, and Communications and Human Relations. Four years later, we decided to revise this curriculum. This time, however, we based our decisions on a more structured set of criteria. First, we needed to consider the long-range plan. In particular, we needed to make sure our management programs were compatible with our Quality Circle (Work Effectiveness) Program. In the Quality Circle Program, participative management is a necessity. Thus, we needed to ensure that our programs taught participative methods to managers. Because group processes are used extensively by our managers, our programs would need to reflect the importance of group processes. Managers would need to use more management skills in contrast to technical skills. Management skills such as delegation and coaching would be necessary parts of our programs. Meetings with the director of Quality Commitment and discussions with consultants were helpful in ensuring that our efforts were compatible with theirs.

In this case, resources were not an issue because we were simply shifting dollars and efforts to a new curriculum. Needs assessment was informal and included a review of the literature on Quality Circles and Work Effectiveness. We decided to enhance the program's marketability by making it a certificate program and offering continuing education units (CEU) to participants. This was in response to our beliefs about incentives that would be attractive to employees.

Judgment played a large part throughout the decision process. Our departmental staff felt that participation in our current management programs was not broad enough. Many of our managers did not attend the programs, although those who did usually felt that all managers and executives could benefit from the experience. In our judgment, changes in program content, the tie into the corporate-wide Quality Program, and the enticement of certificates and CEUs would create additional interest. Because our six-month calendar has just come out, we are still waiting to see if our decision was correct. Another recent decision was to begin career development activities, because career development was compatible with the goals stated in our long-range plan.

A needs assessment was required in order to decide what activities within career development should be given priority. A questionnaire was sent to all employees to identify their perceptions of their current skills, their feelings about their current position, and their estimate of their own promotability. The questionnaire also asked the employees for their specific career development needs, and a computer analysis with various cross-tabulations was run. From this information the five department employees and one University of Wisconsin student identified career development actions (including courses, counseling, and career information availability). Next, to ensure that the decision we made would be marketable, we generated a list of employee objectives from the study and a list of corporate objectives that this curriculum and program would help attain. We assumed that if we met both sets of objectives we would obtain the financial commitment that we needed from the company as well as the participation of our employees.

Using group judgment, we rated these objectives on a scale of 1 to 10 with 1 being the lowest rating. We discussed our ratings to ensure we all had the same interpretation of each objective, and we averaged our ratings. Possible actions were then rated for how well each action would accomplish each objective. (For example, the company objective "To improve utilization of employee skills and talents" was rated 10. The action directed toward accomplishing this objective, "Individual Skill and Talent Assessment," was rated 9. Therefore, the total weighted score for this action in relation to this objective was $10 \times 9 = 90$.) When this action was rated for the nine other objectives, a composite score of 489 resulted. Each of the thirteen actions was rated for the ten objectives, and those total scores were used to rank the actions for implementation priority. The first three in order of priority were (1) training managers in career aiding skills (a coaching and counseling class will be offered), (2) developing a career development center, and (3) offering individual career counseling. As a means of obtaining resources to fully implement these plans, we have compiled the results of our study and our recommendations; if a commitment is not forthcoming, we may shift priorities. This reflects our responsiveness to multiple audiences within the company.

Additional help in making our decisions was gained from visits to other companies to observe and discuss their career development activities. These visits were only marginally helpful because the activities we found were so limited. We joined the Career Development Division of the American Society for Training and Development, but this, too, proved to be of little help. Judgment was the final important factor in the decision. It seemed to us that past participants in our limited career development effort were building their self-images and contributing more to the organization. Personal growth of individual employees is a major source of satisfaction for departmental staff members.

Use of resources was the major factor in our decision to offer more technical, in-house education and training. Our needs assessment involved reviewing requests to attend outside insurance seminars, and, where multiple needs were found to exist, we decided to offer those courses in the company. This is compatible with our long-range planning, though that was not a major factor in our decision process. Marketability in these cases is ensured because the requests specify who would like to attend such seminars. As a result of this review, we decided to offer in-house programs in Accounting Skills and Casualty Insurance.

Conclusions

The five bases that we use for decision making are applied with varying weights in each situation. There is no clear-cut criterion that takes precedence in all situations. It is clear, however, that most of our five criteria apply in each situation. It is also clear that our plan and criteria help managers recognize the rationale for our decisions and help us make decisions that are more consistent and supportable. These criteria have made our decision-making process relatively easy because we do not have to constantly worry about others second-guessing each decision we make. The combination of a rationale and effective relations with company managers contributes to organizational consensus regarding our educational mission. If management support for a proposal is not forthcoming, we may have to withdraw the proposal until we can build necessary support. Without this support, second-guessing would often happen because educators operate in a very visible area—one in which all people feel that they are experts. An explicit rationale for our educational activities has enabled us to establish that we are the educational experts in our organization.

William K. Koeper is the manager of Employee Development for CUNA Mutual Insurance Group. He holds degrees from the University of Wisconsin in risk management and insurance, marketing and marketing research, and continuing education. He has been active in various areas of continuing education for the past twelve years.

No principle is more central to continuing education
than the importance of involving learners in planning their
own programs. The application of this principle, however, raises
some difficult issues.

Involving Adult Learners in Program Planning

D. Merrill Ewert

The belief that the problems of individuals and social systems can be addressed educationally is as old as human history. So are the debates over what should be learned and how it should be taught. Although these discussions frequently assume that defining needs is a methodological concern, the decision to address one set of questions instead of another is a philosophical statement.

Much has been written in the field of continuing education about the involvement of learners in defining their own needs and planning their own programs. The argument for their participation in the process has been made on both empirical and theoretical grounds, but the application of this concept has proven difficult. Although various techniques have been proposed in the literature for involving adult learners in program development, the gap between philosophy and practice is frequently extensive.

This chapter will examine several issues raised by attempts to apply the principle of participation in program development to continuing education programs in several African communities.

Voluntary Associations and Nonformal Adult Education

De Tocqueville's fascination with the American penchant for forming and joining voluntary associations has been shared by other writers. The late

S. Merriam (Ed.). *New Directions for Continuing Education: Linking Philosophy and Practice*, no. 15. San Francisco: Jossey-Bass, September 1982.

Margaret Mead, whose comparative studies of culture have profoundly influenced the field of anthropology, observed that society depends on volunteers and volunteerism. A cursory review of African history reveals that voluntary agencies provided most of the social services in many countries prior to their independence. The majority of the schools, hospitals, dispensaries, training programs, and rural development projects were established not by colonial governments but by missions, churches, and other voluntary agencies. Frequently, these programs became models for the delivery of social services by governments and were sometimes assimilated into the emerging national systems.

The literature generally defines these voluntary agencies in terms of three criteria. First, agencies are organized on the basis of some common interest. Second, membership or participation is voluntary. And third, they are, by definition, independent of the state and control their own agendas.

In his classic study of educational systems, Philip Coombs (1973) distinguishes between informal, formal, and nonformal education. He refers to informal education as the process through which societies socialize or enculturate their young. He defines formal education as the hierarchical, chronological school system that runs from the primary level to the university and includes a variety of specialized programs and institutions involved in technical and professional training. He names nonformal education as the remaining category of educational activity which includes most adult and continuing education programs. Nonformal education consists of organized educational activities outside the established formal system, and these activities are intended to serve identifiable participants and learning objectives.

Voluntary associations have found that nonformal education is the most effective process for addressing the problems of individuals and society. A basic tenet of nonformal adult education is the centrality of participation in the needs assessment and program planning processes.

The Centrality of Participation

The benefits of involving adult learners in defining their own needs and planning their own programs have been well documented. Research has found that this participation results in greater perceived relevance of the educational content, a more favorable attitude toward learning, a stronger commitment to the program, and a greater likelihood that an individual's learning objectives will be met. Experience in the Third World also suggests that this process of participation not only provides a forum for developing educational planning skills, but improves the self-concepts of learners and increases the likelihood that a program will become self-sustaining if the outside resources upon which it was originally based are withdrawn.

Voluntary associations involved in the teaching of adults address this issue of participation at two levels. First, planners are concerned with bringing enough people into educational programs so that the programs' survival is ensured. Consequently, teachers, administrators, and researchers have expended considerable effort in attempting to understand people's motives for participating in continuing education activities. This, it is assumed, will help to focus these programs on the perceived needs of the adult audience. The second level at which the question of participation has been addressed is the involvement of adults in planning their own learning activities. The implications of a high degree of participation in program design have not been well researched and are the focus of this discussion. Specifically, four potential problems will be addressed: (1) adult participation in the teaching and learning process may result in equating an audience's verbalization of a perceived need with an external promise for a programmatic solution to that need; (2) adult participation in program planning may lead to conflict within the existing political system; (3) adult participation in program planning violates the traditional roles of teacher and learner and may cause frustration until the new process is internalized; and (4) adult participation in program planning may threaten the established order (particularly where it reduces the level of dependence upon that order) and cause administrative resistance to effective implementation of that program.

"The Answer Has Come! Come and Get It!"

Ivan Illich (1970) and other social critics have argued that schools have been used by society's elite to manipulate and control the powerless. Freire (1970) refers to this process through which structures not only prescribe actions, but shape the world-views of people, as *domestication*. Convinced of their own inferiority by those who control the structure of power, people view themselves as being subject to the whims of fate and the will of God. People can emerge from this "culture of silence," Freire suggests, by participating in the analysis of their own problems and together developing educational solutions.

Applying this principle to practice, however, is very difficult, particularly within a cultural context of exploitation and oppression. This can be seen in the experience of a voluntary association working in a rural community in Central Africa.

A team of adult educators from a rural development project concerned with agriculture, nutrition, and improved health developed a relationship with a seven-village community over the course of a year. Initial suspicions regarding their motives dissipated somewhat as the team began spraying houses for mosquitoes and bedbugs. This solution to what had been an obvious perceived need led to the establishment of rapport and an invitation to develop an educational program within the community. One member of the program staff took up residence in a central village, while the rest made frequent visits to the area.

With the collaboration of community leaders, meetings were scheduled in each village to identify local problems and to suggest how they might be addressed educationally. It was decided that the initial meetings would define the problems; second meetings would analyze the problems and establish priorities; a third round of meetings would identify educational solutions to the problems and posit strategies for implementation of the solutions in each village. This process, it was assumed, would lead to appropriate teaching and learning activities in which the team would become involved.

The first meetings were well attended, and generated considerable enthusiasm for the process of discussing local problems. Although the list of needs generated through these discussions varied somewhat in detail, several common themes were clearly established: lack of salaried employment, lack of money for paying taxes and children's school fees, low prices paid by merchants for agricultural produce in the community, and exploitation by government officials.

Community meetings to analyze these problems were scheduled three weeks after the initial needs assessment sessions. Again, people came enthusiastically, prepared to participate in the next step of the process. "The answer has come. Come and get it!" said one chief as he called the adults of his village together for the analysis session. "Thank you for bringing the answer to our problems," said another. "We have told you our problems," said a third, "and now we have come to hear how you are going to take them away."

Attempts to involve the village groups in community discussions were frustrated. Bitter accusations that members of the educational team were "playing games" with them replaced the easy camaraderie that had existed earlier. "Why did you ask us our problems if you didn't plan to give us the answers?" several people asked. "Problems do not end with the mouth," others said, quoting a local proverb.

When it looked as if the program staff would be asked to leave the area, a compromise was suggested. Each village, it was proposed, would select several elders to serve as a "development committee," and work with the project staff to implement educational activities to address the problems that had been defined. These committees met regularly to further analyze the problems, to shape the educational content of programs, and ultimately to help teach the educational content upon which the group agreed to focus. This proposed course of action resulted in seminars on how to plant groundnuts and soybeans, demonstrations on the construction of fish ponds, and sessions for women on infant and child nutrition.

An analysis of this attempt to involve rural adults in defining their own needs and planning their own programs revealed several difficulties. The process of asking people to define their problems was considered tantamount to a promise by the educators to solve them. At the same time, it raised unrealistic expectations: some people expected new jobs, higher prices for their agricultural products, and schools for their children. When it became clear that these things would not happen, the tenuous relationship that had been established between the community and the project staff was jeopardized.

Defining Needs in Structural Terms

Freire has focused the attention of continuing educators on the structural origins of social and economic problems. As people become aware of the contradictions in their sociocultural environment, he posits, they will become motivated to take political action to resolve these contradictions. His pedagogy is based on the premise that as communities participate in defining their own needs and developing their own solutions, they will become more motivated to solve local problems. Beginning with smaller, more localized concerns, they will become empowered to address larger and more difficult issues.

The first step in this process is to demystify community problems by exposing their structural causes. People convinced that current problems reflect their own inferiorities and failures are not good candidates for either revolution or educational change. Freire suggests, however, that those who understand how social, economic, and political relationships have limited their own potential are capable of hope that change is possible. The process of reflection and action that he outlines, however, raises some funadmental problems, as an example from another African community reveals.

A community development agent led a village discussion which identified local needs as part of a participatory planning process designed to develop specific educational activities. A listing of economic problems in the community quickly led to an analysis of that country's political structure. Low prices for agricultural goods were ascribed to an official government policy through which farmers, in effect, subsidized the food eaten by their urban counterparts. The Ministry of Agriculture placed ceilings on agricultural products far below their market value and imposed severe penalties on those who violated them. This ensured an adequate supply of food for the cities, which were potential sources of political unrest. Examples of official corruption were noted, and the exploitation of farmers by merchants who worked in concert with unscrupulous politicians was documented.

Linkages between oppressive social structures and local economic problems were established beyond reasonable doubt. The development agent, however, had intended to identify some problems that could be addressed through a community education program. He and his colleagues had then expected to teach farmers how to raise rabbits, improve chicken production, and plant soybeans. The community discussion instead focused on the need for revolution, a totally unanticipated political development in the context of extreme oppression.

Reflection upon this incident later led to one suggestion that the program could generate more lasting changes by distributing guns than by talking about agriculture and health. After initiating the process of examining needs and analyzing local problems, the community development team found themselves involved in something they could no longer control.

Further discussion of the risks involved in such a course of action led people from the village to conclude that nothing could be gained, and that lives could be lost, by pursuing a political solution. They were later proven right when another village that had been involved in a similar community development program in a different region of the country was massacred by government troops. People there had decided to resist exploitation by political leaders (unjust taxes, military roadblocks, blatant theft by government officials, and so on) but virtually the entire village died in a machine-gun attack on the village.

In the former instance, the implications of defining economic problems in structural terms were never adequately addressed. The educational program that evolved focused on food production, nutrition, and health. The local committee, under whose auspices these educational activities were carried out, led further needs assessment discussions and assisted in teaching technical content. Although the educational program did result in some observable improvements in the health and economic conditions in some villages, the understanding that underlying causes had not been addressed was never lost.

Freire has been criticized by many for not coming to grips with the ethical implications of raising people's levels of consciousness through discussion of community problems. Few would now deny that defining problems in structural terms is a political process that might result in putting bullets in disadvantaged people's guns, at least within an oppressive social system. The responsibility for unleashing a process that can potentially exceed controllable limits rests with the adult educator.

Teaching by Induction

Several graduates of agricultural training schools in Africa were engaged to work with farmers on agricultural problems as part of a rural development program. Schooled in the "banking" mode (the traditional method of teacher telling student what to know), the farmers found it difficult to adapt to a preservice training program based upon inductive teaching. Instead of identifying problems and suggesting solutions himself, the training program coordinator focused the first week of the workshop on several questions which were addressed to the community: What are the problems of this region? Why are they problems? What are the underlying causes? How have they been addressed? Why were they addressed in these ways? How do people in the community perceive these problems? What are the ways that adults learn in the village? Which problems have educational solutions? How could these educational solutions be fit into indigenous learning systems?

The initial discomfiture with this approach to training quickly led to the conviction that the trainer was a fraud. Instead of the specialist in adult education that had been promised by the administrators of the project, the participants felt they had been saddled with someone who, they complained, knew even less about the problems of development than they did. Project leaders turned a deaf ear to their protests, so the training program continued with little change.

The first part of the program dealt with conceptual issues surrounding the problems of the region. The second focused on agriculture, nutrition, and health concerns, while the last examined the principles of adult learning within the context of nonliterate rural populations.

The training program included ample opportunity for the participants to practice their teaching skills with various groups of adults. Several experimented with the inductive method, modeled on their own program, while others insisted on lecturing in the same way that they themselves had earlier been taught. Observation of the results was followed by intensive analysis and ultimately led to the conviction that the problem posing (inductive) method was far superior in this cultural context. The rest of the training program was dedicated to sharpening these educational skills.

Although the content of the educational program that evolved included a wide range of practical skills and technical information, the teaching and learning process consistently employed the problem posing method. The educators learned how to listen intently, elicit people's levels of understanding through careful questioning, posit new technical information regarding the subject, and assist the learners in synthesizing previous beliefs with their new knowledge. As a result, the subject matter was kept practical, the pace of learning was determined by the participants rather than the educator, and relationships of trust were built upon the mutual respect engendered by this process.

Not everyone, however, understood or appreciated this approach to the teaching of adults. A highly trained consultant from a European development agency pejoratively labeled these educators of adults "philosophers of development." A program administrator who had observed a seminar led by one of the educators suggested that the educator be given a crash-course on teaching or be fired for incompetence. The training program coordinator who had observed the same session, however, considered it to be the best example of inductive teaching that he had ever seen.

Unfortunately, the tension between those responsible for the teaching and the administrative components of the program was never resolved. One of the issues that emerged in discussions between the two was the image projected by this teaching and learning process. The former felt that it not only demonstrated respect for the audience, but that it was also more effective pedagogy than any of the other available alternatives. The latter, on the other hand, argued that posing questions instead of transferring information compromised the credibility of the educator and decreased the likelihood that the subject matter would be learned.

In this program, several issues were left unresolved. What kinds of content can be learned through inductive teaching when learners have little knowledge or experience with the subject matter? How does one develop teaching skills that build directly upon the needs and concerns of the learners when this is antithetical to their own experience? How do educators responsible for the teaching process carry out their duties effectively when the administrators of the program do not share, much less understand, the premise upon which these are based?

The vulnerability of the adult educators in this example is reflected in a further situation where a consultant was asked to help an agency structure its nonformal education activities.

The Consultant Who "Did Not Know, Either"

An adult education specialist in program design was invited to assist a group of project leaders sharpen the educational focus of a rural development project in another African community by that project's funding agency. The development project addressed agriculture, health, nutrition, and business management issues.

The staff, composed of both Africans and expatriates, had appropriate technical skills in agricultural production but lacked confidence in their understanding of educational principles. They welcomed the consultant with enthusiasm, and after several hours, asked him to outline an educational program that would address the economic and social problems of the region. Instead of immediately providing them with the solutions they requested, he asked a series of questions.

The questions were designed to involve the local staff in the analysis of community problems: What are the problems of this community? How have these problems emerged? What are the underlying causes? Which ones have educational solutions? What priorities should be established? How should these priorities be addressed?

In addition to asking problem posing questions, the consultant facilitated the analysis by clarifying issues, regularly synthesizing the discussion, and providing additional technical information on relevant topics. The frustration level of the project staff was raised by the consultant's refusal to prescribe the means by which the educational program should be established. His explanation that the planning process should be a collaborative venture was met with skepticism. "This man does not know anything about development, either," one member of the local staff told another.

Following a week of planning meetings, the outline of a community education program based on the needs the staff had themselves identified was ready. An analysis of the planning process helped the staff understand how they had been involved in the development of objectives and definition of the educational content of the program. Most then saw it as a model for the kind of process that they should use in involving people in the community in planning. One, however, said, "He really did not help us. This is our plan. We have developed it ourselves."

By any objective indicator, the planning process had been successful. A viable plan of work was established where none had existed earlier. Community problems had been examined, and mechanism had been created for determining priorities. Specific kinds of educational activities were outlined in a program addressing these priorities. Planning and evaluation skills were learned and posited for assessing the effectiveness of those educational activities. The staff felt a clear sense of ownership of the plan as it was developed and subsequently implemented.

The planning process, however, was not as satisfactory as it might have been for two reasons. The participants believed that they had been forced to compensate for the failures of their consultant. The consultant was doubtful that the staff really understood the significance of involving people in identifying their own needs and defining their own programs.

This example suggests that although participatory planning may be good philosophy, implementing it can be very difficult, particularly when those involved do not agree on the value of this premise. Continuing educators must learn how to involve people in planning, yet at the same time communicate technical information: ask questions, but also provide answers in appropriate ways. The alternative is to raise the frustration level of participants and compromise one's ability to be of assistance. It is also critical that those involved in facilitating participatory planning understand local conditions, as is evidenced in the next section.

Solutions That Create Problems

Neonatal tetanus is a major killer of children in Africa. Caused by unsterile conditions at childbirth, the problem can easily be prevented by training midwives to prepare a clean surface for the birthing process, to use a sterile string to tie off the umbilical cord, and to use a sterile blade to cut it. This simple technology is quickly learned and has dramatically reduced infant mortality in communities where it has been practiced.

A community-based health program staff identified neonatal tetanus as a problem and decided to train village level health workers in the use of sterile delivery techniques. Because the village level health workers had been selected by their own communities and had received some basic training in health principles, they were seen as the logical persons to address the problem of infant mortality.

The government, however, not only refused to allow the program to teach midwifery skills to the health workers, but insisted that mothers deliver their babies in hospitals. This request seemed a reasonable solution to infant mortality in the eyes of the government, but many villages were located far from hospitals, and many mothers continued to give birth at home without the sterile conditions that the policy was intended to ensure.

While there was little question as to the nature of the problem, failure to involve people at the rural community level in the search for an appropriate solution led to failure of the policy itself. An outbreak of cholera in the region, however, provided an opportunity for the community health program staff to demonstrate its commitment to improving the health of people and led the government to trust the village level health workers to solve problems at the community level. The training of midwifery skills proceeded, and a significant decrease in infant mortality was realized.

Although this particular incident was, perhaps, unique, the problems faced by educational agencies whose agendas conflict with those of governments are common. Government officials are generally reluctant to involve people in planning and frequently consider such attempts to be subversive. Local control over the content of educational programs may become a threat to the established order, particularly where it reduces the level of dependence upon the society's elite. As a result, the participation of adult learners in planning their own programs may not be possible.

Conclusion

Voluntary associations attempting to address educationally the problems of Third World development face the challenge of application. No value is more deeply held by continuing educators than the premise that people must be involved in defining their own needs and planning and implementing their own educational programs. The translation of this philosophical value into practice, however, is a critical matter.

When attempts to include adults in the planning process are made within social systems that have no tradition of this involvement, it frequently leads to frustration. In situations of oppression where people are excluded from the decision-making process as a matter of policy, their involvement in program development can threaten the established order and lead to further represssion. On the programmatic level, educational organizations frequently struggle with the means for inducing tangible improvement in the quality of life amidst conflicting views regarding the nature of the problem and how it should be addressed. To take the principle of participation seriously and place the learner, not the educator, at the center of the teaching and learning process is to ensure a more effective ongoing program for reasons mentioned at the outset of this chapter. Careful consideration must be given to the issues stated and described above, and more creative solutions bearing on these issues must be found.

References

Coombs, P. *New Paths to Learning.* New York: International Council for Educational Development, 1973.
Freire, P. *Pedagogy of the Oppressed.* New York: Herder and Herder, 1970.
Illich, I. *Deschooling Society.* New York: Harper & Row, 1970.

D. Merrill Ewert is director of nonformal education for MAP International, a relief and development agency in Wheaton, Illinois.

*How are decisions made about resource allocation — budget and staff —
in a large continuing education program with differentiated staffing?*

What's the "Bottom Line?":
Continuing Educators Discuss
Priorities and Values

Gene J. Flanagan
Franceska B. Smith

Continuing education administrators have a curious penchant for appropriat-
ing business terminology. As a group, we are often very partial to phrases like
"cost effective" and "bottom line." We use — and misuse — them, particularly in
conversations among ourselves. One explanation may be found in our tendency to view ourselves as entrepreneurs in a growing, but nevertheless consistently marginal, enterprise. Alan Knox (1981, p. 2) suggests that a widely
shared characteristic is that "the continuing education agency is a dependent
unit of an organization whose main purpose is not continuing education of
adults." Perhaps this explains some of our collective insecurity. Knox notes
further that as a consequence of "the need to attend to both the parent organization and the broader community," many continuing education agencies "tend
to be market oriented, such as business in the private sector" (1981, p. 2). The
organizational effects of marginality have also been documented and analyzed
by, among others, Burton Clark (1958).

      Here in the southern tier of Brooklyn, the continuing education pro-
gram at Kingsborough Community College is large (an annual registration of
approximately 20,000; upward of 250 courses each semester) and well estab-

S. Merriam (Ed.). *New Directions for Continuing Education: Linking Philosophy and Practice,* no. 15.
San Francisco: Jossey-Bass, September 1982.

lished within the college as well as in the community. Yet we are haunted by a sense of marginality. Our management requirements have increased from those of a family owned and operated store of our programmatic youth to those of a sophisticated subsidiary of a corproation (the college), which, in turn, is part of a conglomerate (the City University of New York). In the face of a dilemma, however, the Office of Continuing Education may revert to using an old-fashioned, family business lingo. By so doing, we may appear to be making choices among various action alternatives by the seat of our pants, slighting or even ignoring values as a criterion for decision making.

Of course, there are instances in which we identify and order values explicitly, employ a highly rational approach to policy formulation and implementation, specify desired ends, and then seek the means to achieve them. One example is our decision to recruit skilled practitioners (as distinct from day-school teachers) for our instructional staff as one way of improving teaching and learning interactions. The primary value we identified is our commitment to andragogy; in this instance, we subordinated professional training in teaching skills to demonstrated achievement in a career or skill and to an eagerness to share these skills with other adult learners. Conversations between the dean and his professional staff yielded a clear rationale for the decision, drawing on knowledge acquired from the literature as well as from practical experience with adult learners' needs and interests, teacher competencies, development of nonprofessional teachers, and so on. The effort was delegated to the full-time administrator in charge of staff selection and supervision, who, in turn, works with the part-time evening coordinators at each of our three off-site locations. He sought advice on specific components of the assignment from the dean and other staff members. Such textbook (or formalized) examples of drawing on the professional literature for aid in decision making are also to be found with respect to two other program processes in which specialists are deployed: program development and evaluation. Colleagues in continuing education could supply similar textbook examples from their own experience and would probably add, "If only decision making could always be this straightforward!"

More problematic, however — and more intriguing — are those decision-making dilemmas in which we do not make clear distinctions between means and ends, do not make reference to a fixed or explicit canon of values, and yet manage to achieve consensus on how resources are to be allocated. These judgments are most often, although not exclusively, concerned with budget. Even where money is a secondary concern, we discuss educational policy as a bottom line. This chapter examines the idiosyncratic meanings that our office family attaches to the phrase *bottom line* and how we use this phrase to select priorities that will support our values, even when these values are not discussed.

Excerpts From a Debate

The following excerpts are taken from a discussion that involved the dean of Continuing Education and his inner circle of three full-time administrators. The discussion concerned a series of courses that are proving unsatisfactory by almost any standard. The alternatives are to drop the courses, keep them as they are, or improve them.

- "We could pick up the shortfall by rolling over from some of the non-aidable money-makers. . . ."
- "Well, it may be my Depression mentality, but I don't think I can live with wasting that kind of money — especially on courses with low enrollments and lousy attendance."
- "We might be able to plug up some of the holes and prevent further slippage by holding a special meeting with the site coordinator and the instructors and. . . ."
- "Look, we're going to have to carry these courses until we can beef them up. The bottom line on this one is the political piece — we're running these for the college."

The first and third excerpts are pragmatic remedies, suggesting special allocations of budget and staff. (The time and attention of hard-pressed administrators are scarce resources and, as such, are often more valued than money. The budget lingo will become clearer after we show how it is used within the organization.) The "Depression mentality" referred to in the second excerpt is an allusion to the speaker's memory of having to count every penny in a community-based program because the enterprise had to be self-sustaining. This self-sustaining requirement, if fact, confronts many continuing education programs. Even in programs that receive tax-levy funds, as ours does, spendthrifts do not survive.

In the final excerpt the speaker reminds everyone of the continuing education program's role and status as a dependent unit of a larger, parent organization, and of the obligation to support and promote the missions and goals of the college. This is an obligation we take very seriously; we represent Kingsborough to the community through noncredit programming. This reminder triggered a consensus: The courses would not be discontinued nor would they be allowed to languish as low-quality parasites. They would be improved.

As these excerpts suggest, the bottom line has been deprived of its original meaning through misuse and overuse, although it retains its hard-nosed connotation. As we use it, bottom line describes what is most important, the one priority among several to which we temporarily assign the greatest weight.

Values are implicit in whatever bottom line we select. These values, such as the desirability of a balanced, comprehensive program accessible and responsive to the community we serve, are values which we subscribe to as individual educators and that we generally agree upon as a group. But as Lindblom (1959, p. 328) suggests in a fascinating article titled "The Science of Muddling Through," administrators are buffeted by demands of time and politics. Unable, in Lindblom's opinion, ". . . to formulate the relevant values first and then choose among policies to achieve them, administrators must choose directly among different marginal combinations of values." He argues: "That one value is preferred to another in one decision situation does not mean that it will be preferred in another decision situation in which it can be had only at great sacrifice of another value. Attempts to rank or order values in general and abstract terms so that they do not shift from decision to decision end up by ignoring the relevant marginal preferences" (p. 328).

An overview of the organizational context of our program may suggest why we must attend to so many competing yet interrelated priorities and the values they embody: We must have programs of quality while seeking to maintain and enlarge internal (campus) and external (community) support. These are the constraints and opportunities within which we make decisions about how to allocate budget and staff resources.

Organizational Context

At the City University of New York, continuing education divisions and programs are subject to policies and procedures established and monitored both on the campus level and on the university's central office level. At the university level in particular, and specifically regarding the financing of continuing education, these policies and procedures are also shaped by mandates of city and state legislation and regulations. It is at the campus level — and there are seven community colleges in the City University system — that the purpose and magnitude of the continuing education enterprise are determined. Each college's commitment to continuing education is unique and reflects the nature of the community to be served as well as the purposes and view of the institution. The commitment is expressed through decisions concerning, for example, the allocation of tax-levy dollars to support the administrative costs of continuing education, the distribution of responsibility and authority for noncredit offerings, space allocation priorities, and campus support of such functions as registration and bookkeeping (*Report of the CUNY Task Force on Adult and Continuing Education,* 1980).

Financing Continuing Education. Financing is always a complex issue. In many areas, and with many different types of institutional sponsorship, continuing education programs are required to be entirely self-sustaining or are required to generate profits which must be turned over to the parent organization. Continuing educators at the City University of New York are indeed fortunate that their activities are recognized as meriting institutional support. The City University defines continuing education as noncredit courses and activities that are not part of degree programs, and it includes them as a program element (Extension and Public Service) in the university budget.

A self-sustaining requirement is imposed on continuing education only with regard to the costs of instruction; administrative costs are picked up by each college. That is, administrative staff, heat, light, guard service, and (if necessary) space rental are put on the college's tab, while instructional costs must be covered by continuing education revenues. At community colleges there are three types of such revenues: tuition and fees, grant support, and tax-levy moneys. The only courses that are eligible for state aid are academic, remedial, vocational, or community service in nature or contract courses for business and industry. Those courses identified as recreational, avocational, or social are not eligible for state aid; these are assigned a separate budget.

For both aidable and nonaidable offerings, individual courses need not be self-sustaining although the program as a whole must be. That is, revenues generated from a given course need not cover the cost of that course, but the sum of the revenues generated by the continuing education program should cover all instructional costs incurred by the program. Moreover, whatever their source—FTE reimbursement, tuition and fees, or a combination— revenues in excess of instructional costs (profits) are to be used for continuing education promotion and program development and for general college purposes.

Personnel Selection and Deployment. This is another area in which continuing education administrators at City University enjoy considerable latitude. Instructors are hired on an hourly basis; there is a minimum rate of compensation (currently, about $20.00 per hour regardless of length of service) but no ceiling on rates of compensation or number of hours. Instructors may be credentialed specialists, experienced classroom teachers, or proficient practitioners. The title of Continuing Education Teacher was created in recognition of the distinctive role of continuing educational instructional personnel. (These teachers have no research commitment or participation in campus committees and no review by the college's personnel and budget committee.) They are hired, evaluated, and fired by continuing education administrators.

Other part-time positions include supervisory personnel who usually manage evening off-site programs or coordinate a particular outreach program. Independent contractors may also be hired to provide professional services or short-term, special programs. Most of these part-time staff members are paid by revenues generated by the Continuing Education program; failure to meet projected revenues means reduction of this staff.

Full-time staff are paid from the college's tax-levy budget. They include the dean, three full-time administrators, and several secretaries. The college also hires and pays for administrative support personnel: secretaries, clerks, and typists.

The interrelation of budget and staff is illustrated by the consequences of shortfalls (failure to meet enrollment and revenue projections). For a self-sustaining program, a shortfall spells deficit and possibly demise. For a tax-supported program, it spells disruption of program priorities that depend on deployment of part-time staff. On the other hand, when times are good and Continuing Education is generating more FTEs than projected, we can make up a "shopping list" (new staff, new telephones) to take to the college president.

Does the Bottom Line Work?

Given the organizational context within which our program functions and given the size and complexity of our enterprise, decisions to make extraordinary commitments of resources cannot be made routinely and, moreover, must be made collectively and quickly. There are rules of thumb but no formulas for pitting budget and staff against a problem (such as an unanticipated shortfall) or committing them to a new programmatic thrust (for example, developing courses for new client groups such as business and industry). Identifying the bottom line—that is, specifying the highest priority in a given decision situation—and organizing policy around it is one method of allocating resources.

As with continuing education programs in many other settings, we have multiple obligations: to our parent organization, to our clients and community, and to our own profession. The tax-levy support we receive removes the burden of being entirely self-sustaining but imposes an additional obligation: We are part of a public institution and share responsibilities of public service. However we choose our bottom line, it usually centers on one of the following obligations which overlap, compete, and sometimes conflict.

- *Program Quality and Viability:* The two may be combined as, for example, in decisions to keep tuition low to promote volume (revenues) and to ensure that program offerings are financially accessible to our constituents.
- *Internal Considerations:* Often we attend to strengthening internal (college) support for continuing education (for example, decisions to assist in recruitment for credit programs).
- *External Support:* Promoting external (community) support for continuing education and the college and City University is an important consideration. We like to think that our entire noncredit program is a form of community outreach; we also contribute staff expertise to community development and civic associations.

The challenge in selecting the bottom line is to design policy so as to avoid preempting subsequent priorities, whatever they may be, and to achieve the best possible combination of values—what Lindblom (1959) terms "adjustments at a margin." A bottom line is not immutable. As a priority selected for extraordinary allocation of resources, the bottom line changes with the program over time, as conditions and aspirations change. Our method of identifying a range of competing priorities and choosing the bottom line relies more on experience than on theory, more on comparison of anticipated outcomes than on formalized decision-making theories. In the course of our graduate training as continuing educators, none of us in the Office of Continuing Education has yet found a theory or formal strategy sufficiently comprehensive to encompass all alternatives (and precise enough to describe them) or sufficiently specific to our situation to be relevant. Nor have we found in the literature of adult and continuing education a conceptual framework of values that satisfies our desire for comprehensiveness, precision, and relevance. It may be, however, that the process of seeking—the reflection and debate in which practitioners engage—is an important endeavor in itself and that the professional literature can guide that search.

References

Clark, B. *The Marginality of Adult Education.* Chicago: Center for the Study of Liberal Education for Adults, 1958.

Knox, A. B. "The Continuing Education Agency and Its Parent Organization." In James Votruba (Ed.), *New Directions for Continuing Education: Strengthening Internal Support for Continuing Education,* no. 9. San Francisco: Jossey-Bass, 1981.

Lindblom, C. E. "The Science of Muddling Through." *Public Administration Review,* 1959, *19,* 79–88.

City University of New York. *Report of Task Force on Adult and Continuing Education.* New York: City University of New York, 1980.

Gene J. Flanagan is dean of continuing education at Kingsborough Community College and former principal of the Sheepshead Bay Adult School, both in Brooklyn, New York. He has a doctorate in higher and adult education from Teachers College, Columbia University.

Franceska B. Smith combines motherhood with consultant work for Kingsborough's Office of Continuing Education and is completing her doctoral dissertation in higher and adult education at Teachers College, Columbia University.

The word juggle *indicates the tension inherent in limited resources and heavy time constraints. It also hints of the tension between theory and practice — knowing and doing.*

Continuing Education Administration: A Juggler's Task

Carolyn Farrell

How does one plan, implement, and evaluate a continuing education (CE) program in a small, liberal arts college? Energetically!

The challenge to define and meet adult needs in a small setting requires personal commitment to the concept of lifelong learning, enthusiasm for the task, and a sense of the "extra mile." These three factors enable a director of continuing education to develop a program within limited resources and heavy time constraints, and to meet the needs of adults in a local area.

To educate women and men wisely we must know what we educate them to become. We ask: What is the purpose of life? What should life be like? What is the nature of the world and its limits? These initial questions are the tip of the philosophical iceberg supporting education.

In a discussion of continuing education, these same questions surface. The process of program development presupposes a philosophical base for the practical initiation and implementation of continuing education programming. The CE program at Clarke College is built on concern for the person. A philosophy of education creates an atmosphere for adults to become authentic persons who have the right to choose to continue their education even though they are older than twenty-two or work forty hours a week. This concept of

S. Merriam (Ed.). *New Directions for Continuing Education: Linking Philosophy and Practice,* no. 15. San Francisco: Jossey-Bass, September 1982.

education moves beyond the traditional approach of an eighteen-to-twenty-two-year-old pursuing a liberal arts education at Clarke. At times, the philosophical stance supporting concern for person is sorely challenged by the established system. The following account of Clarke's CE program attempts to reflect program development in the real world setting of tension between theory and practice.

Clarke College was on the cutting edge of the back-to-school trend of the early 1970s. As a women's college, Clarke had college administrators who recognized the growing women's movement and hired a part-time person to meet those needs. A grant proposal was written and partial funding was received from Title I of the Higher Education Act of 1965, to establish a women's center at Clarke. This center was one of the first in the state of Iowa. The action also launched the continuing education program at Clarke.

At the same time, the college created a full-time position, director of Special Programs and Summer Session. As such, I have participated in the establishment of a strong and viable part of the college. It was a delight to be able to say that CE was in on the ground floor at Clarke and in the state of Iowa.

Living through the process, it was difficult to anticipate the outcome. In retrospect, it is encouraging to note that commitment produced a new dimension in an institution of higher educational characterized by quality education.

Today, the Division of Continuing Education consists of a full-time director and secretary, with a part-time assistant responsible for student services. This organizational pattern is a definite part of the institution but was not an arbitrary process. The steps taken in 1972–73 led to the establishment of the CE division as an integral part of the college.

As the director of the CE division at a small college, I am charged with many tasks all wrapped up in one: successful delivery of education to an adult population. As an administrator, I must wear many hats or, as a juggler, keep many items in the air. The major areas of responsibility include program planning and implementation, finances, public relations and promotion, student services, faculty relationships, and administrative detail. Where does one begin? Which task is first? Where does it lead? What happens if it fails? Who are the key people to know? How is success measured?

I believe that choosing where to begin reflects the motivating force of the person in charge. A strong concern for person motivated me to develop for potential participants a process which would enable them to grow intellectually, emotionally, and spiritually. I belive that adults are creatures of feeling as well as intellect, and in order to know something, they must be able to relate it to themselves. Knowledge must be joined to the true goal of the adult, which is to become authentically involved with life. The beauty of this truth fades in my consciousness as the practical how-to rises to the surface in a necessary first step of needs assessment.

The CE administrator must decide on a process to assess local needs. The identification of educational needs is critical for large scale development, such as the implementation of a CE Division within a college, as it is for small scale development, such as a one-day seminar for working women. This is the first step in all planning.

During this particular era of declining traditional age enrollment, there is a real tension between philosophy and practice in the area of program development or recruitment. A solid CE program must be built on the foundation of the institution. That is a hard struggle at times. Pressure may come to recruit students in order to maintain a stable headcount while little thought is given to what the institution has to offer the students. It is the responsibility of the person in charge of the program to ask the hard questions: What do we have to offer adult students? Will it meet their needs? What do we need to change within our institution — while maintaining its mission — to meet those needs?

At Clarke College, during the CE developmental stage, a number of activities were initiated to assess needs. I chaired a committee of faculty members whose task was to recommend a course of action for program planning in the area of continuing education. In one action, the chair of the economics department guided one of her classes in developing and implementing a telephone survey of the Dubuque area. The survey was designed to identify educational needs, times of delivery and tuition constraints for adults. Meanwhile, the Higher Education Facilities Commission of the State of Iowa conducted a study, "Postsecondary Planning for the Nontraditional Learner in Iowa" (1976). The study required college response to a statewide questionnaire and a personal interview with the director of the study. The state planning brought together CE representatives for the Regent Institutions, the private colleges and universities, and community colleges to reflect upon statewide planning needs. The state's concern for the adult learner highlighted our own recognition of the nontraditional student and the needs of the local area. As Clarke's study committee was at work and the state's committee was drawing up its recommendations, it became clear that Clarke had another factor to consider in planning for adult students: local institutions of higher learning.

Since there were two other colleges in the city and the institutions strove for Tri-College cooperation, continuing education became an area for cooperative planning. The CE directors of the three colleges realized that one institution would be unable to mount a full fledged evening degree program designed to meet adult needs. Working together, the three schools could schedule a variety of courses on a rotating basis to meet degree requirements. Such planning would schedule existing course offerings so that student needs would be met, duplication of efforts avoided, and curricular gaps filled. The enthusiasm of the directors for a unique, academically sound degree program designed for adults faced the practical problem of convincing faculty of the need for and value of this approach to liberal arts education. The tension between our theory about adult needs and the practical implementation of college life for adults is highlighted by the fact that the administrators are only in the position of facilitating the process of learning between the adult student and faculty. They have little control over faculty thinking or their approach to teaching, in areas of either content or style. The cooperative program planning initiated by the directors provided the advantage of three administrators working together, rather than a single office struggling in isolation.

As a result of the needs survey at Clarke, the recommendations of the state study: "Lifelong Learning in Iowa in the Third Century" (1977), and work with Loras College and the University of Dubuque, Continuing Education at Clarke took its first steps beyond a Women's Center and toward becoming an integral part of the institution.

Three major outcomes resulted from the needs survey. First, adults returning to college to finish or begin their degrees preferred evening or day classes; a weekend college was not suitable for this area. Second, nearly 60 percent of those wanting to enter college were women. Third, business courses were listed as high priority. The needs had been identified. The ongoing process of planning, implementation, and evaluation began. For the CE administrator, meetings were top priority in the total process. Their functions varied from detailed planning to general CE consciousness-raising.

There were many meetings held at the state and regional levels. These meetings related to the total operation of a continuing education program. The meetings provided needed linkage with neighboring institutions, other public and private institutions within the state, and local civic and business organizations. The ongoing problem for a small institution is the valuable time spent attending such meetings, this time that might better be spent in the planning or implementation of programs in process.

I personally believe in the value of attending off-campus meetings because they offer linkage and visibility to the small liberal arts college. They provide the opportunity to receive insights from others and to share our own, and thus provide leadership. The returns in public relations and direction setting are great. However, the meetings create real time pressure. The discussion often centers around the philosophical base for continuing education, but ultimately it is the practical how-to that draws us together. I think it is important to recognize the significance of these meetings in relation to the CE administrative responsibilities within the college and to allocate time accordingly.

Meetings also took place in conjunction with the other two institutions involved in the Tri-College program. It became clear, through meetings with the other two Dubuque colleges, that a cooperative B.A. degree program would best meet the needs of the adult learners of the area. Weekly meetings with the Tri-College task force over a period of three years brought forth the Tri-College B.A. program. The task force consisted of the directors of CE at all three institutions and one other member of each institution. The task force was committed to establishing a program to meet the needs of the adult learner within the Dubuque area. Prior to this there was no degree program for students who were only able to attend classes at night. Essentially, it was not a new degree program but a repackaging of current course offerings in such a way that adult students could attend classes in the evening and earn a degree from one of the three colleges. Admission requirements were designed for the returning adult, and a reentry seminar was structured as part of the degree requirements. The major offered was business, with core courses for all students, and built-in flexibility for the degree-awarding institution for specific departmental requirements. This is called the art of compromise.

Besides the weekly Tri-College planning meeting, Clarke had its own CE planning committee. As the director, it was my function to set the agenda for planning, based on the perceived needs of the local community. The challenge of leadership in a new area of the college was both exciting and frustrating. A CE program had never been developed before, so a "blue sky" approach was possible. Traditional faculty and administrative offices, however, questioned the why and how of a program oriented to the nontraditional student. Emphasis was placed on the development of the Tri-College B.A. program, but daytime CE needs were also studied. Student services surfaced as a concern. Noncredit programming was discussed. It was a challenge to keep both of these committees moving forward. Others on campus were not directly involved or committed to the notion of lifelong learning. Some faculty did serve on the study committee, and they seemed most interested in the adult learner. These faculty members shared the belief that formal learning has a place in the lives of adults. It could be said that their theory of education supported the new practice being introduced to meet the needs of a new student population.

Parallel to the Tri-College committee work, the Clarke CE committee studied the academic needs of adults and realized that a reentry seminar was necessary for adults returning to school. Adult students were concerned about their ability to compete with younger students. They also lacked confidence in their study skills and seemed to need the encouragement and support of peers for a successful beginning in the academic setting. Conversations with potential participants supported these findings. With this background, the committee formed a subcommittee of faculty members to design a reentry seminar. Long hours of extra work resulted in the first adult student seminar in the city, at Clarke. It was offered as a pilot program in 1977 with a faculty team of five members. The goal of the seminar was threefold: skill building, an overview of the liberal arts, and a sense of a support group in the college setting. In time, this seminar was introduced into the Tri-College program and was the foundation of today's reentry seminar.

With the development of the reentry seminar, I had to be concerned about faculty involvement, budget, and promotion. The details necessary for this offering, ranging from course listing with the Registrar to an evaluation form, originated in my office. Given the institutional budget, the seminar was not a top priority for funding. The faculty's strong belief in the value of the reentry seminar motivated them to carry the project as an overload with minimal reimbursement. This commitment, together with the support of the CE office, provided the necessary impetus for a successful project.

Two years later, the Tri-College committee developed and received a National Endowment for the Humanities grant entitled, "The Individual in Transition." Project goals were designed to assist adults returning to an academic setting. The grant helped to fund the development of an improved re-entry seminar and three area courses for the Tri-College B.A. degree program.

With the academic content set, it was important that the program be promoted. With careful planning, the Tri-College committee was able to obtain a $25,000 promotional grant from the Wahlert Foundation. This funding enabled the colleges to hire a quarter-time person to promote the campaign.

In 1977, three major events happened that heightened the work load in the CE area. They were (1) the approval of the Tri-College B.A. program by all three Dubuque colleges, (2) the creation of the Division of Continuing Education at Clark by the Board of Trustees, and (3) 40 percent enrollment of adult (over age twenty-four) students. The task of academic planning continued, but with the increase of potential students for advising and actual students on campus, the need to identify and to serve students needs surfaced as top priority. With the creation of a division of continuing education, an administrative shift took place and a part-time assistant director was appointed. Her major task was to coordinate student services in the area of advising and campus life.

In the early days of the women's center at Clarke, a woman could register for college work without test scores and recommendations. This practice of easy access was further developed for returning adult students. It has come to mean that a man or woman can call for an appointment or walk in off the street for free advice regarding a possible college career. This service is time-consuming but it is the practical application of our belief in the principle of availability for students. It is a deliberate choice of office policies to reflect our concern for person by reducing the barriers for adults returning to college.

Adult needs vary. Therefore, I occasionally function as a counselor. Meeting potential students has reinforced my concept of individual differences within the adult student population. I vividly remember talking with one woman who was in the middle of a personal crisis. After twenty years of marriage to a minister, she learned that he was leaving her for another woman. She had married right after high school and since then had played the organ at church functions, kept the books, made cookies for the socials, to say nothing of having children and caring for their home. She was beside herself. She could not get a job because she had no work experience. What was she to do? I felt angry and limited in my response to her personal needs. I did listen, which is part of our work, did suggest some possible jobs for her in the city, and explained to her the first steps toward beginning a college education.

That woman represents many who come to our office looking for advice after a divorce, death of a spouse, or midlife blahs. It is our philosophy of service to the returning or beginning student to listen, analyze strengths and needs, and then advise. Counseling is a time-consuming task but one that serves the students and in turn, the institution.

With the influx of CE students as part-time or full-time students came the need to make the process of registration and advising flow smoothly into the registrar's office. Clarke is a small institution, and the computer system did not include our office in its program. This issue raised another administrative problem to solve with the registrar's office and computer center. Forms had to be designed to help adult students move through the necessary red tape without too much frustration. Adjustments had to be made down to such small but important items as making sure that the "parent" would not be labeled as receiving the bill or report card.

As the program grew, other services were needed. At first, a small room on the lower level of a classroom building served as a CE lounge. Students asked for more space, a refrigerator, and a clock. Today, the lounge is a bright, airy room on the first floor in the center of the building, complete with a refrigerator, clock, and stove. We also supplied mailboxes and lockers. At first, babysitting was offered. However, the service was evaluated, and various financial and legal complications caused us to eliminate it. The concept remains, however, in our five-year plan for possible refinement and implementation. A CE newsletter, the *Continuum,* is a regular feature of the division; it is written by the assistant director as an informational piece and is designed to incorporate adult students into the total college community.

The various facilities of the college, such as the Student Union, swimming pool, and tennis courts, are available to CE students. A strong effort has been made to include them in the college community. Since adult students differ from other students in the degree that they want to identify with college life, we strive to provide a variety of options for them. Their time is limited, but they appreciate the availability of facilities and services.

Service also means providing a supportive atmosphere for CE students. Answering the telephone in the absence of my secretary, I was asked to give a message to a woman in the CE lounge: "Please pick up Elizabeth's homework at the front office of Washington Junior High and good luck with your test. Your husband." Delivering the message spoke in a small way of our support, but it spoke volumes about student life as a CE student.

Financial aid, critical to all students, was another challenge for our office. We could tell the basic facts regarding financial aid, but the financial aid office handled the application process for state and federal grants and loans. Once again, we worked in conjunction with another office in the college to inform them of our students' needs and to support its work in any way we could.

Further help in funding CE students for college was received from a Title III grant. Through the grant we were able to identify employers of the area who gave tuition reimbursement. This information helped us in our planning and advising of students. The CE office also looked for other sources of funding for CE students.

Another source of grant money was the college itself. As the CE administrator, I pursued such a possibility for two years. During that time, I studied financial aid policies of other private institutions. I had to make a strong case for need with college administrators. The business office and financial aid committee finally listened to our request for a dollar amount to be allocated for tuition assistance for CE students. Guidelines were developed and approved by the appropriate committees for the awarding of some tuition assistance to those students who demonstrated need but who could not qualify for state or federal assistance. The two year process sufficiently raised the consciousness of the administrators of the college concerning CE financial need so that the 1980 budget contained $2,000 with $7,000 allocated in 1981 for the beginning of institutional financial aid for CE students.

For me, the financial hat of the administrator's role takes a great deal of time and is the most frustrating aspect of the job. The first item of concern is the office budget, which is just one part of the academic vice-president's total plan for academic programming. The line items are clear in the definition of specific items supporting the office of the CE division. The crunch comes in justifying additional funding for a growing program or division. Time is spent wrestling with the dollar amount needed for CE promotion and publications. That item is a part of the public relations budget, but it is my task to suggest, argue, or demonstrate the need for an increase in the projected amount for our division.

It is my challenge to present the necessary rationale to support or reach nontraditional students through the existing structure of budget and budget guidelines. Most faculty and administrators think only of the eighteen-to the needs, concerns, and behavior of the eighteen-to-twenty-two-year-old stu- anyone but bright-eyed coeds and broad shouldered athletes. They do not consider adjusted bookstore hours or advising times. Some of these items require budget adjustments. The belief in adult students must exist before structures can begin or be changed.

A second item is to present adult population concerns to the advisory council to the president, a group that reviews the projected increase in tuition and fees. What type of increase will they be able to pay? How much is too much? Is it fair to pay a student fee when the services are designed for the traditional age student?

In response to the latter concern, the CE Council, advisory to the CE Division, studied the question of student fees for over a year. In the end, they recommended to the budget committee that full-time CE students pay half of the student fee for full-time students and part-time students pay half of the fee, or one quarter of the assigned full-time student service fee. The final decision rested with the budget committee.

By necessity, the CE office is limited by institutional constraints. The budget process, tied into five-year planning, requires many meetings at different levels of the institution before the total package appears on the table before the Board of Trustees. The size of the institution necessitates the same people meeting at different times looking at fiscal responsibility in the light of program needs, faculty needs, and other institutional needs. This process creates an awareness of strong, overall institutional dollar needs and constraints. I find myself the witness to CE needs at the various committee meetings. For me, their need is my top priority. It is my voice that says: Don't forget the CE students. My stance at those meetings supports my philosophy of concern for person and the freedom for adults to choose a college education, although they are beyond the traditional age. The challenge is to represent CE fairly and to know when it is best to compromise and when it is important to press on for program needs.

Financial concerns are also part of every CE noncredit program that is offered. A budget is necessary for each offering. Projected revenue and expense are estimated and plans are implemented. This, too, is a time-consuming task but one that becomes easier with experience. Necessary financial guidelines have been developed by the CE office to implement noncredit programming. They do not guarantee successful programming, but they provide insurance in case of failure.

During the development of the Tri-College B.A. program, a recommendation was made to keep fees and tuition the same at each one of the participating institutions. This decision of the Tri-College planning committee was approved by the three business offices. This joint commitment is another result of cooperative planning.

Faculty involvement with CE students and programs is coordinated through the CE office. In the early development of CE planning, faculty in-service was initiated. Speakers were brought to faculty meetings to talk about the needs of adult learners. The challenge of a mixed age group was openly discussed with faculty. In most cases, CEs were enrolled in the regular class offerings. Only a few courses were limited to or designed solely for CEs. The process of educating a CE awareness was slow but beneficial; most faculty enjoy CEs in their classes.

From my perspective, such in-service is a valuable part of the development of a functional CE Division. Most faculty members are accustomed to the needs, concerns, and behavior of the eighteen-to-twenty-two-year-old student population. It is necessary to remind faculty members of the uniqueness of the individual, with specific abilities and limitations, as applied to the nontraditional age student. I have the same concern for person as I prepare a program for the faculty. It is important for me to realize that faculty, too, have different needs. The process of consciousness raising regarding adult needs should not be a threatening but a positive experience for the faculty.

Faculty members have served on CE planning committees and on the CE Council. The linkage with faculty is necessary and good. It provides the give and take for an honest working relationship which supports quality programming.

The most recent faculty CE committees studied the question of credit for prior learning. The committee reviewed current literature describing credit for experiential learning and the guidelines used by various institutions to award such credit. Committee members also attended workshops explaining implementation procedures. They struggled with the local CE need to award academic credit as well as the development of appropriate guidelines to ensure a valid learning experience. The final outcome was the approval by the Educational Policies Committee of the proposal to award credit for prior learning.

In approaching the faculty regarding this topic, I took a low-key but persistent approach. The faculty places a great value on learning within the context of an academic setting. Quality of course content is important to them and academic credit is looked upon with high esteem. They are fearful that awarding academic credit for life experience weakens the academic learning process. Philosophically there is a difference between education as a product and a process. As the product, education is what we receive through learning. As a process, education is the act of educating someone or educating oneself. Credit for prior learning forces this discussion to take place.

In my position as director, I have not taught any classes, although the assistant director has taught the Adult Reentry Seminar and will teach one of the National Endowment for the Humanities core courses. I have presented various noncredit programs. In a small college, it is helpful for administrators to have many skills, and teaching is one of them.

Another important skill is promotion. With limited funding, free publicity is a must. Again, this task begins in the CE office. Each offering is promoted within individual budget constraints. Public Service Announcements are used. Speaking engagements are taken by CE administrators to spread the message regarding continuing education at Clarke. Trends in CE are watched and studied. Brainstorming sessions are held to search out new ways to share our programs with the adult population.

Currently, general college material reflects the presence of CE students on campus. This change has taken place due to consciousness raising by the CE office. We continue to support a total college community but it is our task to remind our colleagues that adults and part-time students are part of that community.

Today CEs are an integral part of life at Clarke. The juggler's act has been part of the seven years' work to accomplish the task. Amidst all the activity, three underlying factors have been critical in my administration of this program. First, a deep belief that adults have the right to try for a college education; second, determination to see a project through to completion; third, ability to compromise or offer alternative suggestions. The three factors work together to reinforce the value I place on educational opportunities for adults. Beyond my personal beliefs were the support of the president and my administrative style.

Five years ago, Dr. Dunham began her term as president of Clarke. From the moment she arrived, continuing education was identified as an important area of the college. Her previous experience as a dean had put her in direct contact with a strong women's program in Continuing Education. She witnessed a good program and saw great merit in it. The notion of a good CE program stayed with her. With her support, the college established the Division of Continuing Education. This division became visible and began to function as a viable part of the college. The student body had a "new look," and it was officially recognized.

The process of planning and implementing as previously described was accomplished with the encouragement of the president. The support was no more than the verbal commitment to lifelong learning and the recognition of its value in an academic setting. In a small college, that support was very important. It provided the needed push on the days when time seemed short and money thin. Part of the support came in the freedom I was given to plan. Such freedom did not remove all barriers or frustration, but it provided the space for productive administrative work.

As the administrator, I have the freedom and responsibility to allocate time to the various tasks associated with CE as I judge necessary. It is important not to waste it on minor details or fail to delegate work to others when it is important to do so. Thinking time is necessary, but given the daily pressures, such time is often found riding alone in a car to a meeting or walking across campus. The time given to meetings is important, but the time given to planning for meetings is as important. The effective use of time is the sign of good organization, and this is a must in a small college.

Good organization leads to the final factor in my success: well-defined office staffing. Service is clearly the goal, the backdrop for the daily implementation of office objectives. The objectives of each position are clearly stated regarding the workload. However, each person in the office appreciates one another's work. This creates an atmosphere of mutual ownership in the division. Stability of personnel has allowed each to grow in her knowledge in the field of continuing education.

The spirit provides a degree of flexibility for operations within the office. Energies can be directed to the top priority of the day or week without a great deal of stress. The secretary is well able to act as a personable back-up advisor when needed. She can answer questions and meet the public in ways that demonstrate the philosophy of service. But most of all, beyond relational skills, she is able to manage an office in a steady way, which enables the administrators to accomplish the tasks at hand.

Without personal beliefs, well-defined office staffing, careful use of time, and the support of the president, the juggling could not have stayed in motion. Juggling is the external movement reflecting internal thinking. It represents the practical actions needed to implement a CE program. The word *juggle* indicates the tension inherent in limited resources and heavy time constraints. It also hints of the tension between theory and practice — knowing and doing.

58

The practice is seen in activity; the theory is present in discussion. The CE program at Clarke is built on concern for person. The various parts of the process, beginning with the advising of potential students through my struggle with budget guidelines, reflect a philosophy of education that creates an atmosphere for adults to become authentic persons with the right to make various choices regarding their education in a liberal arts college. Our goal continues to be the practical implementation of programs that reflect our theoretical concern for person.

References

Educational Testing Service. "Third Century: Postsecondary Planning for the Nontraditional Learner." A report prepared for the Higher Education Facilities Commission of the State of Iowa. Princeton, N.J.: Office of New Degree Programs, College Entrance Examination Board, Educational Testing Service, 1976.

McLure, G. T. "Recommendations for Lifelong Learning in Iowa in the Third Century." The Final Report prepared for the Higher Education Facilities Commission of the State of Iowa, September 1977.

Carolyn Farrell is director of the division of continuing education at Clarke College, in Dubuque, Iowa. She currently serves on the Iowa Coordinating Committee on Continuing Education.

Instructor evaluation in adult basic education is viewed as an extension
of staff development. Primary emphasis is upon improvement rather
than rating of teacher performance.

Teacher Evaluation and Staff Development in Adult Basic Education (ABE)

Edward V. Jones
Jean H. Lowe

For the most part, administrators who evaluate teachers focus either on rating teacher performance or on improving it. This is not to suggest that most administrators are interested in only one of these areas but rather that evaluation procedures inherently and inevitably reflect one intent at the expense of the other. In most instances, we believe that the appropriate choice for adult basic education (ABE) administrators is an approach oriented toward staff development and improvement of teacher performance.

Although performance ratings may lead to improved teaching, instructors know that the purpose of performance ratings is to gather data pertaining to personnel decisions (assignments, promotion, salaries, rehiring, firing, and so on), and they tend to regard such evaluation methods as adversary proceedings. As a result, the emotional climate surrounding this form of evaluation rarely supports the type of open communication between instructors and administrators and among instructors themselves that is conducive to improved teacher performance or to increased achievement of program goals. Even positive ratings may be ultimately damaging to morale because they

S. Merriam (Ed.). *New Directions for Continuing Education: Linking Philosophy and Practice*, no. 15.
San Francisco: Jossey-Bass, September 1982.

reinforce the threat of judgment and imply the necessity of maintaining a high level of performance as measured by external standards.

We do not intend to suggest that there are no valid purposes for teacher ratings; in some educational settings with large numbers of employees, these may be the only means available for making personnel decisions. The point is that teacher ratings are used primarily for administrative purposes unrelated to the improvement of teacher performance.

After grappling long and hard with this issue in both theory and practice, we are firmly convinced that teacher improvement should be the focus of evaluation. Our viewpoint is based on experience with the nature and goals of adult basic education, on the qualities we have observed in adult education teachers, on teacher effectiveness research, and on an andragogical view of the adult learner.

Adult basic education teachers are often part-time employees who work at difficult and challenging jobs in relative isolation from other teachers and administrators. If teachers are to improve their own abilities to meet student needs, they need open, nonthreatening communication with administrators and with their peers. Each instructor must be encouraged to seek help from others and to evaluate and modify teaching practice as appropriate. Rather than being judged by external standards, often an impracticality to begin with in highly individualized ABE classrooms and learning centers, teachers need to make instructional decisions based on the needs of their own students consistent with overall program goals. They will do so most effectively in a climate which emphasizes sharing rather than judgment. And they will do so by thinking about what they are doing with their students and how they might do it more effectively.

The contention that ABE teacher evaluation is an integrated phase of staff development is more than theoretically sound; it can be applied in practice. In the remainder of this chapter, we will address both the supporting rationale and the means of implementation for an approach to ABE teacher evaluation which is primarily designed to improve teacher performance in the context of program goals.

Philosophical Perspective and Supporting Rationale

The view that teacher evaluation in ABE is best conceived as helping teachers to improve their effectiveness is supported from several vantage points: (1) the nature and goals of adult basic education, (2) the background and qualifications of ABE teachers, (3) the research into the characteristics of effective teachers and (4) the andragogical view of adult education.

Nature and Goals of Adult Basic Education. Adult basic education is defined in federal legislation as remedial education for those adults who have not completed high school. Adult basic learners struggle to cope with a variety of literacy demands imposed upon them by their living and working environments, and their resulting educational needs vary widely from student to student. Learning programs, including goals, methods, materials, and schedules must therefore be negotiated separately between each student and the instructor. Because student needs are so diversified—one individual may want to read the newspaper and write letters to her children, while another may need to read his work orders or safety regulations on the job, and yet another needs to compute sale prices—they can seldom be addressed entirely through the use of any existing curriculum. The instructor must diagnose each student's needs and collaborate with that student in the design, implementation, and evaluation of an individualized instructional plan that becomes the initial phase of an ongoing and highly personalized teaching and learning process. Accordingly, evaluation of the student should not be a mechanism for comparing one student's performance with that of others, but a rediagnosis of learning needs resulting in revised goals and a new plan of instruction.

Such individualized instruction in adult basic education has an impact not only upon the purpose of ABE instructor evaluation but upon the process also. It is hardly appropriate, for example, to compare student pre- and post-scores on standardized tests as a measure of teacher effectiveness when the standardized test items in any particular instance are no more than tangentially related to either the student's or the teacher's objectives. Furthermore, because test-taking is not a coping skill required of ABE students in their living and working environments, most conscientious teachers do not spend much time in sensitizing students to test-like items or to the experience of test-taking itself. In addition, evaluating ABE teachers on the basis of student improvement in standardized test scores might corrupt the teaching process; teachers would be reluctant to recruit and retain the federally mandated target group, those "least educated and most in need," a group characterized by previous school failure and difficulty with standardized tests. Encouraging teachers to cream the top level of students to enhance their own performance ratings is hardly in accord with the established ABE mission.

Equally unsound is the practice of evaluating teachers on the basis of student satisfaction. In ABE, the teacher-learner relationship, regardless of teacher effectiveness, is likely to be characterized by deep affection. When they experience their first academic success, ABE learners tend to think that their teachers deserve the credit. On the other hand, if they fail, they blame themselves, because after all, they feel, they have always failed. Because negative comments are unusual, it would certainly be useful to hear student criticism of teaching behaviors, but approval is not sufficient evidence of effective instruction because of the learners tendency to idealize their teachers. Student attendance, completely voluntary in all nonmilitary, noninstructional ABE programs, may be read as a more accurate measure of student satisfaction than self-reports, but economic, health, child care, and personal problems affect the ABE population disproportionately, resulting in uneven attendance regardless of instructor performance. While high attendance levels and measurable student achievement reflect favorably on teachers, the absence of these factors is not necessarily significant.

Background and Qualifications of ABE Teachers. ABE teachers are as unique as their students. Unlike elementary and high school subject teachers, they do not have to fulfill specific certification requirements in most states. Although many public school divisions (or other agencies sponsoring ABE programs) require that ABE teachers be certified in some area, a particular instructor's endorsement may bear little relationship to ABE subject matter perhaps because so few training programs exist to prepare ABE teachers. Although there is certainly a need for university courses and other forms of training to sensitize teachers to the adult remedial learners and the ABE environment, the absence of specific subject matter certification requirements is perhaps justifiable. As we have said, adult basic education, by definition, is remedial education, focusing on basic literacy and math skills and everyday coping skills which most adults perform routinely as a part of their daily lives and work. As a result, no particular academic preparation is essential for ABE instructors. Instead of specific content endorsements and specializations, administrators who hire ABE teachers are more apt to seek the sorts of personal qualities which would best enable prospective instructors to communicate effectively with undereducated and often otherwise disadvantaged adults. In addition, administrators look for background that suggests the levels of patience, tolerance, respect for cultural differences, and genuine interest in the student necessary to teach these individuals for extended periods of time.

In short, ABE teachers are hired primarily on the basis of personal qualities and interest rather than academic credentials and professional background. Ideally, of course, the successful applicant is well qualified in all these areas. In addition, adult basic education, due to precarious budgets and uncertain enrollments, usually offers only poorly paid, part-time, and often insecure employment, which is nonetheless challenging, demanding, and fatiguing. ABE teachers are employed in part because they are considered to be sincere and conscientious, and their perseverance under difficult circumstances reflects these qualities. It seems reasonable then that the focus of evaluation be on improvement, not judgment.

Research on the Characteristics of Effective Teachers. Just what are the qualities that make a teacher effective? Instructor performance has been assessed in a variety of ways and correlated with the measurements of any number of dependent variables (attendance records, learner perceptions, learner test results, learner accomplishments after the fact, and so on). Nonetheless, researchers have failed to identify any meaningful patterns of instructor methods or characteristics consistently associated with effective teaching. Malcolm Knowles, in his book, *The Adult Learner: A Neglected Species* (1973), refers to the work of several investigators who have reviewed the substantial numbers of teacher-performance studies over periods of as much as forty years and concluded, essentially, "that practically nothing seems to make any difference in the effectiveness of instruction" (p. 89).

Other writers, Gage (1972) and Mouly (1973), based on their own reviews of the literature, suggest that there are certain personal and "relationship" qualities associated with effective teachers, for example, warmth, enthusiasm, effective communication, patience, empathy, emotional stability, democratic and cooperative attitude and so on. Obviously, such lists of varied attributes do little to describe teacher effectiveness conceptually. They suggest only that good teachers possess many of the qualities necessary for forming good relationships or for becoming good friends. These observations are neither surprising nor helpful. It goes almost without saying that ABE teachers lacking human relations skills would be as ineffective as those who had not mastered basic skills. But these qualities fail to distinguish effective from ineffective teachers. The lack of general agreement about which attributes distinguish good teachers makes teacher evaluation even more difficult.

How then can ABE teachers be evaluated with an emphasis on improvement of teacher effectiveness? The focus of this effort, we believe, should be upon helping teachers to assess and continually reassesss their own learning needs in a manner that helps them to grow personally and professionally — and improves the effectiveness of the overall ABE program as well.

The Andragogical View of Adult Education. The theory of andragogy, which provides an appropriate conceptual framework for addressing the learning needs of ABE students, is also an ideal perspective for addressing the learning needs of instructors in evaluation. Teachers, like students, will achieve their best growth in a supportive climate which provides the opportunity for open collaboration and mutual problem solving.

The term *andragogy,* as opposed to pedagogy, refers to a body of theory which has emerged over the past few years. As elaborated by Malcolm Knowles and others, it sets forth at least four assumptions about adults as learners which differ significantly from the assumptions typically made about children as learners in the areas of self-concept, the role of experience, readiness to learn, and orientation to learning.

As individuals reach psychological adulthood, andragogy assumes, they develop a need not only to be self-directing but to be perceived by others as self-directing. Andragogy emphasizes the use of the learner's own experience as a resource for learning and interactive techniques which allow the learner the opportunity not only to share with others but to use his or her broad base of experience as a foundation to relate to new learnings. As observed by Knowles (1972), this base of experience not only distinguishes the adult from the child but is crucial to the adult's self-concept in the learning environment: "A young child identifies himself largely in terms of external definers—who his parents, brothers, and sisters are, where he lives and to what school and church he goes. As he matures, he increasingly defines who he is by his experience. To a child, experience is something that happens to him; to an adult, his experience is who he is. So in any situation in which an adult's experience is being devalued or ignored, the adult perceives this as not just rejecting his experience, but rejecting him as a person. Andragogues convey their respect for people by making use of their experience as a resource for learning" (p. 35). Furthermore, andragogy assumes that adults learn best what they themselves want to know as opposed to that which someone else tells them they ought to know. And finally, andragogy assumes a time perspective of immediate application. Because they want to apply tomorrow what is learned today, adults typically approach learning with a problem-centered orientation.

The implicit view of teaching apparent in most traditional pedagogical environments is that the instructor bears the full responsibility for the development of lesson plans and the transmission of content. Proponents of andragogy, preferring the term facilitator to teacher or instructor, view the facilitator's task not as one of dispensing knowledge, but as one of nurturing and guiding a mutual but primarily learner-directed inquiry. Learners become personally invested and take a major role in designing their programs and evaluating their own progress. Knowles (1972) has suggested a seven-step process through which the facilitator may serve as a resource to the learner. The elements of this process can be summarized as follows:

1. Creating a climate conducive to adult learning. (A climate emphasizing informality, mutual respect, physical comfort, and collaboration—as opposed to competition—openness, nondefensiveness, trust and curiosity.)

2. Involving all learners in the development of the learning plan in which they will participate.

3. Diagnosing needs (a process through which facilitators help learners identify and compare present and desired levels of competence).

4. Formulating program objectives (collaboration between learner and facilitator).

5. Planning a sequential design of learning activities (collaboration between learner and facilitator).

6. Conducting the learning experiences (management of the processes of interaction between the students and the resources for learning).

7. Evaluating the learning (rediagnosis of learning needs).

The authors concede that this andragogical model may not apply to all types of adult learning situations. For example, in the military, education is primarily for the benefit of the institution. The needs of the individual are secondary, if not incidental. In addition, the content of some adult education programs is so specialized that a true collaborative mode is impractical. Since neither of these factors applies in ABE, we believe andragogy is the most appropriate model for instruction, although it is not widely implemented.

Knowles' seven steps constitute an ideal model for assessing and improving teacher performance in ABE as well as for teaching ABE students. The assumptions implicit in andragogy are that teachers, like students, want and can learn to improve their effectiveness and have an immediate need to do so; that they have experiences which can serve as resources to themselves, other teachers, and program administrators; and that they can and will formulate objectives for their own improved performance. The model also assumes a climate conducive to learning, as Knowles (1973) wrote: "If every learning experience is to lead to further learning, as continuing education implies, then every evaluation process should include some provision for helping the learners reexamine their desired competencies and reassess the discrepancies between the model and their newly developed levels of competencies. Thus repetition of the diagnostic phase becomes an integral part of the evaluation phase" (p. 122).

Administrators who advocate that instructors treat learners in this manner must treat instructors accordingly. Instructor evaluation should have a teaching and learning function which challenges teachers to reexamine their own goals and teaching methods and to make the adjustments that they consider appropriate. This does not mean, of course, that administrators and program directors have no input into this process. Their roles are discussed in the following section.

Strategies for Implementation

The philosophical perspective for ABE teacher evaluation described in the preceding section can be implemented through combined use of three evaluation and staff development strategies which are equally appropriate for classrooms, learning centers, and other ABE instructional settings: (1) biased questionnaire, (2) peer observation, and (3) case study at staff meetings. We recommend that these strategies be employed as an integrated package.

Since we have identified the purpose of instructor evaluation in ABE as "the effort to help teachers improve their effectiveness within the context of program goals," it is important that our strategies for implementation be consistent with all aspects of this intent. We have emphasized that administrators should afford teachers the ongoing opportunity to reassess their own learning needs in a climate which is conducive to professional growth. This does not imply, however, that administrators should not attempt to influence the nature of this development. Adult basic education supervisors, like all administrators, are responsible for providing direction to overall programs. ABE administrators have both the prerogative and the responsibility to encourage that instructor attitude and performance be compatible with program goals.

Nonetheless, while retaining primary responsibility for program direction, administrators must avoid stifling communication. As student needs change, ABE programs should evolve to meet these needs, and, in order to make informed decisions, administrators must gather information from as many sources as possible. They cannot afford to be closed off from what teachers are thinking. The integrated use of the three strategies below is intended, therefore, to encourage the professional growth of ABE teachers in a manner consistent with program goals while promoting open communication between teachers and administrators and among teachers themselves, so that these goals do not become rigid and inflexible.

Biased Questionnaire. At first glance the biased questionnaire is simply a form for ABE teachers to fill out, supplying certain basic information for an administrator's files. This form, which can be officially titled something like "Program Inventory — Staff Questionnaire," asks each instructor fill-in-the-blank questions covering educational background, training in adult education, professional memberships, and community activities which might provide resources for ABE. After gathering demographic information, the biased questionnaire asks open-ended questions, designed to encourage teachers to reflect on the teaching process, their own professional growth, and then to structure the teaching and learning environments in accordance with program values and needs. Questions are phrased in terms of *how* goals are pursued, not *if* they are.

Although the biased questionnaire can be designed to address a variety of program issues, our preference is to group questions into the following categories: professional development, instructional program, climate for learning, space utilization, instructional strategies, student recruitment and retention, community resources, and job satisfaction. A few examples of questions in each of these areas reflect the biases of the authors.

Professional Development:
1. What have you done to foster your own professional growth in the past year?
2. What plans do you have for the coming year?
3. Which in-service sessions were most helpful?

Instructional Program:
1. How do you design a student's instructional program to meet individual needs, interests, and goals?
2. How do you make initial testing less threatening?
3. How do you include the student in the evaluation process?
4. How do you combine the student's life experiences with his or her academic work?

Climate for Learning:
1. How do you make the learning center's atmosphere warm and accepting?
2. How do you encourage students to help each other?

Space Utilization:
1. How is the room arranged for student interaction?
2. Is there a quiet place?

Instructional Strategies:
1. How often do you use various instructional methods? (Accompanied by a list and scale of frequency.)
2. What materials have you developed that you could share with other teachers?
3. What strategies and materials have you found most effective?

Student Recruitment and Retention:
1. What do you do to recruit new students?

2. What help do you need and what help could you give others?

Community Resources:

1. What community resources have you used this year?
2. How did you learn of these resources?

Job Satisfaction:

1. What do you like about your work? Dislike?
2. What are your strengths as a teacher?
3. In what areas do you need help?

We recommend that an instrument with questions of this type be distributed to all teaching staff at the beginning of the school terms with instructions to return it at mid-year giving them ample opportunity to reflect on how to arrange and to improve upon their instruction in accordance with program goals and values. They can seek assistance as needed from supervisors, other teachers, and students. Most important, they are encouraged to think about what they do instructionally and why they do it — as opposed simply to following a set lesson plan or curriculum guide.

In addition to its usefulness for staff development purposes, the biased questionnaire serves a purely evaluative function as well. Not only are teachers exposed, at least indirectly, to the ideas and values of program administrators before they start to work, but after reflecting on the issues raised by the questionnaire and experimenting for some months in their own teaching, they are forced to express their own commitment (or lack of commitment) to these values. Administrators then, in visits to classrooms and learning centers, can observe the extent to which this commitment is reflected in teaching practice.

For many ABE teachers, the questionnaire has provided the opportunity to brag about their considerable accomplishments. Typically they report having fun in completing it, often discussing the questions in terms of "I never thought of...," "How could I learn to...," or, "I didn't know that I should be doing this, but I will now." They also express their own needs for administrative support. "I wish you would..." They express concern about their weaknesses as well as their strengths and set specific goals for themselves. "Next year I'll...."

One point needs further elaboration. Teachers need not present detailed evidence of having implemented all of the instructional ideas suggested by the biased questionnaire. In fact, an individual teacher may disagree with some of these ideas or prefer other techniques and materials. This is fine — provided that the individual is basically in sympathy with program goals or can state his or her reservations about administratively supported goals, methods, and materials and is willing to share and to demonstrate his or her preferred methods and materials to the rest of the staff. In this manner, the biased questionnaire serves not only as an instrument for staff development and evaluation but as a device to promote intrastaff communication as well.

Use of the biased questionnaire is consistent with the philosophical perspective at the beginning of this chapter. If ABE teachers are to be encouraged to individualize instruction for their students, they must be given the opportunity to document and to share the methods and materials they have employed. Furthermore, the biased questionnaire promotes a spirit of collaboration and exchange of ideas among teachers which not only helps to develop the relationship qualities known to be associated with effective teaching but is itself consistent with an andragogical view of adult education. Through use of the biased questionnaire, teachers continually assess, address, and reassess their own professional learning needs in a problem centered orientation requiring immediate application of learning progress. Another way to encourage staff interaction is by peer observation.

Peer Observation. Few professionals see as little of their peers in action as teachers. This situation is unfortunate; peer observation among instructors offers tremendous potential, not only for nonthreatening, no-cost evaluation but for staff development as well. In general terms, we propose the model outlined below.

All ABE instructors would be paid for a designated amount of time (perhaps 5 percent of total work time) during which they would be assigned to observe the teaching of their peers. This could be organized in several ways. One workable arrangement would be for each teacher to exchange visitations with perhaps three other teachers of his or her choice over the school year. Although individuals could handle these observations in any manner which was mutually agreeable, we have found one approach to be particularly successful. According to this format, each observer would record a list of student and teacher behaviors and activities. For example, this list could include such entries as: "talks to left side of the classroom more than right," or "worked with Mrs. A for twenty minutes, Mrs. B for ten; Mr. C worked alone in corner; two students corrected math workbook together; gives some students in the learning center more attention than others," and so on. At the conclusion of each exchange visitation, the observer provides the observee with a list of statements or phrases similar in form to the example above.

It must be stressed that the items on the evaluation list are to be stated in a value free manner. Not only is the observer nonjudgmental but often does not know whether the observed teaching behavior was intentional or not. In the case of the example above, it might be that the instructor has made a conscious decision to speak more to some students than to others. Perhaps the classroom or learning center is arranged so that students needing the most guidance are located in one area while students who are more independent are seated in another. On the other hand, the instructor may be unaware of this discrepancy and wish to modify his or her teaching practice. In any case, the observer's function is to reflect what he or she sees, not to pass judgment or give opinions unless requested to do so in follow-up discussion.

It is important to emphasize that peer observation is a two-way street which benefits the teacher-observer as well as the teacher observed. In addition to providing an information "mirror" for his or her peer instructor, the observer benefits from seeing a fellow teacher in action. What better way to expose oneself to new instructional ideas than to observe the manner in which another instructor implements them in the classroom or learning center? Follow-up discussion of these activities then serves two additional purposes: it not only broadens the teaching perspective of the observer, but also provides an ice-breaker which may allow the observed instructor to feel more comfortable about discussing other teaching behaviors which are recorded on the peer observation list.

The peer observation procedure is a successful technique for no-cost evaluation. It is nonthreatening in the sense that no decisions are made as a result (except the individual's own decisions about modifying his or her own teaching practice), and no reports are made to administrators about teacher performance. At the same time, peer observation provides an excellent opportunity for instructors to share ideas and serves as a catalyst to facilitate intrastaff communication.

As indicated at the beginning of this chapter, ABE teachers are assumed by their employers to be sincere, conscientious, perservering, and interested in helping others. Peer observation puts these qualities to good use. Further, it promotes the supportive climate for mutual problem solving which is emphasized in the andragogical view of adult education. Teachers not only receive valuable insights but model with their peers the type of collaboration they need to develop with their students.

Staff Meeting Case Study. The third segment of our proposed staff development and evaluation program is the staff meeting case study. This activity might appropriately occur twice during the year—at the beginning and at the end—and would provide an opportunity both for administrators to acquire insight into how different teachers approach learners and for teachers to share these insights with each other.

In the case study activity, each teacher at a staff meeting would present an in-depth description of a particular adult learner followed by an account of strategies developed (or proposed) to diagnose and address that student's weakness. Other teachers then share their reactions, emphasizing those ideas that they support and those which cause them hesitation. All teachers benefit from this exchange while administrators acquire insight into the thinking of individual instructors and stimulate their own thinking with respect to program goals and staff development needs.

The staff meeting case study provides a final opportunity for collaborative problem solving in a supportive learning environment. Because ABE students require highly individualized learning programs and substantial creativity on the part of teachers, pooling of insights and resources is desirable.

A Few Afterthoughts

At the beginning of this chapter we stated our belief that instructor evaluation in adult basic education should be focused primarily upon improving rather than rating teacher performance. As a result, our approach to the assessment of teacher performance has been directed at helping those teachers who are already doing a good job to be even more effective.

For some time prior to writing this chapter, we discussed our ideas on ABE teacher evaluation and staff development with other adult educators. A typical response has been something like: "All right, you've made a convincing case for how one should think about and implement ABE teacher evaluation under most circumstances, but what would you do about teachers who are obviously not doing a good job. If you were to discover, for example, or perhaps to inherit, a teacher who was condescending to students, rigid in attendance requirements, used to a high school approach, or whatever, what would you do as an administrator? How would your evaluation system work in firing a poor teacher?"

These are good questions; it is certainly true that our system has not been primarily designed to help administrators deal with teachers who are "obviously not doing a good job," since we believe that very few ABE teachers fall into this category. Nonetheless, we believe that our system is appropriate for assessing and dealing with this problem — more appropriate perhaps than most approaches to teacher evaluation.

If the administrator feels that the instructor in question is not teaching effectively within the context of program goals, it is for one of two reasons: (1) the teacher does not accept the principles and values upon which the program is based or (2) the teacher does accept these principles and values but is unable to implement them in his or her teaching practice.

The biased questionnaire is especially helpful in identifying possible discrepancies between the instructional principles and values which guide the work of a particular instructor and those which support administratively determined program goals. Staff meetings, case studies, and resulting discussions are also useful for this purpose. In cases where discrepancies are found to exist, biased questions further provide a basis for individual discussions between teachers and administrators which may be helpful in clarifying and resolving these differences. When these issues cannot be resolved, and transfer or termination must be considered, the biased questionnaire provides data which document areas of disagreement.

In the majority of instances, of course, teachers do not disagree with program goals since, if they did, they probably would not have been hired in the first place. Problems are more apt to arise in the area of implementation. In this situation, the biased questionnaire is most helpful when followed by an administrator's visit to the classroom or learning center as discussed earlier. Teacher and administrator can then analyze discrepancies between values and performance and how these can best be corrected. As follow-up to these discussions, peer observation then affords an instructor the opportunity to observe other teachers as they employ more appropriate strategies and materials, and to receive additional feedback on efforts to improve performance. In this manner, the struggling teacher is provided not simply with a performance assessment but with a support system, which in many instances leads to a quick and dramatic increase in teaching effectiveness.

Teachers who are unable to improve under these circumstances seldom wait to be fired but resign of their own accord. In those rare cases where termination becomes necessary, this administrative decision can be supported with ample documentation.

Conclusion

At the beginning of this chapter we stated our belief that teacher evaluation in adult basic education is a phase of staff development. The intent of ABE instructor evaluation, we emphasized, should be to help teachers to improve their effectiveness within the context of program goals. After an extended discussion of the supporting rationale for this viewpoint, we presented an integrated package of three strategies designed to implement such an evaluation procedure.

The focus of our evaluation approach is upon the instructor's ongoing rediagnosis of his or her own learning needs. The greater the extent to which administrators encourage and facilitate this process, the more teachers will grow professionally, and ABE programs will improve accordingly.

References

Gage, N. L. *Teacher Effectiveness and Teacher Education: The Search for a Scientific Basis.* Palo Alto, Calif.: Pacific Books, 1972.

Knowles, M. S. "Innovations in Teaching Styles and Approaches Based Upon Adult Learning." *Journal of Education for Social Work,* 1972, *8* (2), 32–39.

Knowles, M. S. *The Adult Learner: A Neglected Species.* Houston: Gulf Publishing, 1973.

Mouly, G. J. *Psychology for Effective Teaching.* New York: Holt, Rinehart and Winston, 1973.

Edward V. Jones is in-service coordinator at George Mason University, Fairfax, Virginia. He has been active in a variety of staff development activities in adult basic education and is the author of Reading Instruction for the Adult Illiterate.

Jean H. Lowe is coordinator of adult basic education and GED programs for Fairfax County Public Schools. She is responsible for staff and curriculum development for one of Virginia's largest ABE and GED programs.

Only philosophers are purists. When philosophy systematically and consciously informs practice, practitioners do not operate in a world that conforms to their assumptions. In the arena of practice, the educator must negotiate philosophy.

Contradictions in the Practice of Nontraditional Continuing Education

Phyllis M. Cunningham

Should every adult have access to a college degree? Should we uproot our schooling system because it does not always work? Should we get rid of credit, which increasingly serves as the basis for a credentialing society? Should we place the responsibility for learning in the hands of the adult learner rather than in educational institutions? Should we recognize that education is political and has as its end either a liberating or a domesticating function? These are some of the questions that educators face and answer, often without an awareness of their philosophical stance.

Adult and continuing education had a rich history of debate about its purposes and goals. Illustrated by such instructional forms as the Junto, Chautauqua, and Great Books program, a strong courrent of liberal thought among continuing educators has held that the purpose of continuing education is to build a better society by helping people to become better informed. However, some recent opinion holds that as continuing education becomes more and more institutionalized, its ends and effects are increasingly becoming those of socialization or domestication. Moreover, a form of anti-institutionalism has taken root; this can be loosely classified as nontraditional

S. Merriam (Ed.). *New Directions for Continuing Education: Linking Philosophy and Practice*, no. 15. San Francisco: Jossey-Bass, September 1982.

education. This movement, which began about fifteen years ago, exhibits some features that have long existed in one form or another but now appear with renewed vigor.

To explore this problem, the social and political forces that gave rise to this movement will be identified, three types of nontraditional education will be suggested, and some conflicts that emerge within each type will be outlined. Next, conflicts between theory and practice will be examined in these three types, and finally, the uneasy future of the nontraditional adult education will be discussed.

Social and Political Forces for Change

A constellation of factors caused the rapid development of nontraditional education in the last fifteen years. First, there were several problems occurring in higher education in the late sixties. The rapid growth of higher education led to widespread abuses in which the means (colleges and universities) seemed to become ends, thus contributing to unrest among student bodies, some of which contained significant numbers of returning mature students. The dehumanizing effects of large classes, seemingly impersonal faculty-student relationships, and the power of the computerized registration and regulating process conflicted with the ideals of educational purpose which held the student to be of primary importance. Student and public challenges to academia combined with two other forces: the aging of the population base and the demand for access from minority groups encouraged by new civil rights legislation. These two forces increased the flow of adults back to the campus and put pressure on higher education to adjust curricula and services to fit a more mature, culturally pluralistic student body.

Women also began returning to campus, many after long absences. Some were drawn back in response to the women's movement; others were pushed toward schooling because of single parent status or the need for two incomes in the family.

Critiques of schools as political institutions and schooling as a political process also intensified during this period. In this country, such futurists as Toffler (1970) questioned the purpose and relevance of schools. In Third World countries, critiques of schooling as a means of oppression were being articulated and acted upon. The ideal of deschooling society was embraced both by humanists, on the grounds that individual potential was being blunted or truncated by schools, and by radical educators, on the grounds that schooling oppressed individuals by maintaining and enforcing power relationships in the society.

The educational experiments of Freire (1970) in Brazil profoundly challenged the system of schooling not only in less industrialized countries but in postindustrial societies as well. This country, with an awakened and growing nonwhite underclass, was also challenged because it required increasing education to gain and keep a job.

The impact of technology on the work place increased levels of education required for job entry, offered the potential for several changes of occupation during a life span, and increased the need for updating professional knowledge. This force also put pressure on the higher education system to respond to adult student needs.

This confluence of social events put pressure on the system of traditional education to make changes. Internal adjustments were made to provide more openness at the undergraduate level, on the assumptions that credentialing was appropriate and that the major problems were access and quality curricula. The higher education establishment adjusted in another area as well. Recredentialing the already credentialed emerged as a new field of endeavor for the university. A new type of credit, the continuing education unit (CEU), was invented; this development appealed to a new clientele, those seeking continuing professional education. Contradictions in practice resulted: opening up the credit system for adults at the undergraduate level while imposing a credentialing system on professionals.

These two responses within higher education were viewed both positively and negatively by continuing educators. Some educators, who for years had been advocates of extension and special adult degrees, saw these nontraditional efforts as directly supporting their philosophy and practice. They quickly exploited the situation to provide further access for adults to credit and credentials. These educators also developed qualitatively distinct curricula based on the adult's greater range of experience. Still others brought together the "free university" idea, which resulted from campus rebellions of youth, with the growing interest in naturalistic and spontaneous learning of adults. Still another modest but growing number of continuing educators eschewed the ideal of reform of the credit system and worked to provide educational programs based on the belief that schools were destructive and that an entirely new set of assumptions were needed to build an education system. This group attacked the idea of opening the credit system to professionals through the CEU as a lethal extension of the credit system to continuing education. Adult educators with a similar critical analysis of schools and society concentrated their efforts on freeing the underclass through liberating approaches to education in which the power imbalance was explicated. These educators sought to redress the power imbalance by empowering individuals through a dialogical process of education.

In summary, broad social forces such as demographic and value shifts, civil rights efforts, increased identification by racial/ethnic minorities and women as an underclass, and political movements within the Third World affected the views of many Americans on the purpose and functions of schools. Schools, under pressure from these attacks on traditionalism and highly exposed in terms of their limitations, were ripe for reform. Continuing educators, responding in terms of their own philosophies, attempted to either liberalize or reformulate the system. To see how these ideals were translated into practice, the definition of nontraditional education and resulting forms will be examined.

Definition and Distinctions

The most complete definition of nontraditional education is that suggested by the Commission on Nontraditional Study (1973, p. xv) which states:

> ... nontraditional study is more an attitude than a system and thus can never be defined except tangentially. This attitude puts the student first and the institution second, concentrates more on the former's need than the latter's convenience, encourages diversity of individual opportunity rather than uniform prescription, and deemphasizes time, space, and even course requirements in favor of competence and, where applicable, performance. It has concern for the learner of any age and circumstance, for the degree aspirant as well as the person who finds sufficient reward in enriching life through constant, periodic, and occasional study. This attitude is not new; it is simply more prevalent than it used to be. It can stimulate exciting and high-quality educational progress; it can also, unless great care is taken to protect the freedom it offers, be the unwitting means to a lessening of academic rigor and even to charlatanism.

This definition recognizes the growth of both credit bearing and credit free alternatives. The most pervasive type of nontraditional continuing education is the credit bearing form, which accepts the ideas of credit and credentialing but focuses on the issues of access and a unique curriculum for adults. The educational alternatives that are free of credit are often included in this definition conceptually, even though there are very few restrictions in programming in which credit is not awarded. What is not included in this definition is a type of alternative program with a distinctive philosophy that is antithetical to the rigidities of schooling and has the personal empowerment of the learners as a primary goal. Thus, there emerge from this definition two types of nontraditional programs: credit bearing and free form (credit free) to which is added a third type, personal empowerment, which is not included in this definition. Simpson (1977, p. 2) has conceptualized nontraditional education as education that potentially varies components, such as time, place, method, as shown in Figure 1.

Free form education would be at the far left on these continua. Credit-bearing nontraditional forms would be found in the middle area as a negotiated form of traditional education. Personal empowerment types of nontraditional education are not represented in this model.

Figure 1. Non-traditional/Traditional
Program Characteristics Continua

	Individual Orientation Determined exclusively by the student	Mutually determined by the student and institution or program	Institutional Orientation Determined exclusively by the institution or program
Time	Students select when learning activities will take place.	———+———	An arbitrary time is pre-scribed by the program or school.
Location	Student selects place of learning activities.	———+———	School or program site used only.
Method	Student selects method best suited to his/her style of learning.	———+———	One method selected and used by the program.
Content	Student selects what is to be learned.	———+———	A specific, single cur-riculum is prescribed by the program.
Objectives	Student provides own objectives.	———+———	Objectives established by program or institution.
Evaluation	Student evaluates his/her own performance to measure progress in meeting objectives.	———+———	Evaluation is conducted by the program in meeting program objectives.

Non-traditional —————————————————Traditional

Credit Bearing Education

This nontraditional form of education for adults is by definition institu-tionally (school) based, since its aim is to provide credit or degree oriented education. Components might include open entry, self-pacing, differential timing (weekend college), alternative curricula (competency based degrees or individualized contracts), assessment degrees (no campus, no courses), and distance learning (TV, radio, newspapers, correspondence). The hybrids are myriad as educators in universities, colleges, and high schools seek ways to create access to credit and degrees for adults.

Free Form Education

This more anarchistic approach minimizes institutional organization and is disinterested in, if not opposed to, institutional credit. It includes indi-vidual learning projects as described by Tough (1971), free universities and learning exchanges as described by Draves (1980), and community scholar-ship programs as envisioned by Gross (1980). Such institutional trappings as prerequisite hours, certified teachers, credit, and approved curricula are con-sidered unnecessary if not harmful. "Anybody can teach and anybody can learn" is a basic concept. Learning is a natural human activity and the idea that learning should be enjoyable is emphasized. The autonomy of the learner is sacrosanct in this type of education; any institutional base for assisting learners should be minimal and activities should be facilitative rather than normative. Learning is a social activity but the relationship of teacher to learner is devoid of status and is one of learner reciprocity. The objectives, design, implementation, and evaluation are in the hands of the learner.

Personal Empowerment Education

This is a political collective (group) approach to the best way of educating adults. Suspicion of institutions is shared with the free form educators but it is not limited to schools, since the adult learner is seen as oppressed by societal arrangements that define people as objects and thus as disenfranchised. The goal of education is first to assist the learner to free him or herself from this oppression, to demystify knowledge, and to allow the prevailing social reality to be redefined by the student. This process of demystification and the redefinition of social relations by the adult student leads to personal empowerment and the ability to apply a critical analysis to society. Nontraditional approaches are found in community based educational programs (which may have loose and often tenuous institutional ties) or such free standing programs as the Highlander Folk School (Adams, 1975). The teacher's role is facilitative, the teacher's task is to arrange a curriculum generated from the "reality of the learner," a curriculum that increases the learner's capacity for critical analysis of society in terms of his or her own social reality.

The proponents of these three nontraditional approaches tend to be drawn together around the issues they have in common. At the same time the basis for and extent of their critical analysis make them uneasy partners. All three types of nontraditional educators seek to place the learner at the center of educational practice and to actively work against the institution (school) as an end in itself rather than a means of serving students. Each approach seeks to enhance struggles with the right of the individual to full accession of opportunities for learning for his or her own direct benefit and for the direct or indirect benefit of society. To study the nature of the conflicts engendered in practice, one must turn to an analysis of the conflicts within each type.

Conflicts of Philosophy With Practice Within Types

Financing Issues. One major conflict between theory and practice that occurs within both the personal empowerment and free form nontraditional adult educational program has to do with financing. If one's educational philosophy challenges traditional institutions, one can expect resistance almost in direct proportion to the threat posed. Since schools, both in secondary and higher education, are in large part supported by public funding, an excellent way of resisting reform is to deny financial resources to alternative schooling.

Financal resources are essential since no nontraditional educators suggest that educators or facilitators should work for free and since community based organizations and learning exchanges or free universities clearly require funds for facilities and materials. Many of the educators in both these institutional types contend that they should have access to public funds since the adults served are taxpayers. This argument is most cogent for personal empowerment programs, which for the most part, provide services to adults who have had minimal educational opportunities. Many of these community based programs are helping adults below the secondary level. Federal law, and at times state law, guarantees public money for support of such programs. Traditional schools and their systems, however, have been markedly successful in denying them public funds, and access to facilities and materials.

Some of the educators employing the personal empowerment model refuse to dissipate their energies in seeking public funds and rely on foundation support, private donations, or fees to sustain their activity. Examples are the Highlander Folk School and St. Mary's Alternate Adult High School of Chicago (Heaney, 1980). One could argue that schools based on the empowerment model, which could legitimately seek public funds and do not, contradict their own philosophy of redressing power inequities. On the other hand, one could also argue that the freedom to concentrate one's energy on the practice of one's philosophy and to keep free of accountability to a system regarded as corrupt (by accepting public funds) is a more consistent expression of that philosophy.

Free form nontraditional continuing education is not generally perceived as a threat to traditional institutions. These programs have received federal funds (for example, University of Man, Kansas) or shared the facilities of a university. However, in times of diminishing public resources for education, it seems clear that the need of traditional institutions for these minimal funds could erode even the minimal financial support available to the free form educators. Securing financial support from public funds has therefore been an issue for personal empowerment programs (and a perennial concern for free form programs). The extent to which leaders of such programs modify their philosophy in order to survive financially will affect their impact. For example, the recent movement of the original Learning Exchange in Evanston from the Northwestern University campus to shared facilities with an entrepreneurial variant of the free form type in the center city may markedly diffuse the Exchange's goals. Can free and mutual exchange of learning to encourage human potential exist side by side with an institution with a markedly different philosophy?

Credit bearing nontraditional programs have financial issues, but not in the same way as the other two types. The issues of financing for credit bearing nontraditional programs arises from intrainstitutional competition for funds. It is hard to define the motivation of administrators of traditional institutions in introducing nontraditional credit bearing programs. The rhetoric is uniformly one of increasing access, responding to needs of adult clientele, attacking the problems of rigidity, and other laudable objectives. In practice, however, many nontraditional credit bearing programs exist on the margin of the budget and outside of the main administrative structure and its powerful enclaves. Accordingly, the alternative programs often have less money for their curricula, and personnel in these programs often lack the security of full-time tenure track positions. Although financial deprivation does not apply to all credit bearing alternatives, it is characteristic of many, if not most, programs. Again the traditional program's personnel guard their resources.

The Credit and Credential Issue. In the personal empowerment type of nontraditional education an inconsistency between theory and practice can also be observed in terms of credit and credentialing. Philosophically, these educators view the credit and credentialing system as a part of the oppressive system of traditional education. They believe that credit and credentialing limits access to institutions, encourages the codification and mystification of knowledge, and encourages status differential for elites. This leads to "old boy" networks and self-protection for those within the system. However, students among the poor and minority racial or ethnic groups, as well as women, aspire to those credentials and in fact need them to obtain employment. Many of these community-based programs are developed as alternative methods of gaining the high school credential or its equivalent. Is it not inconsistent, or at least unwarranted pragmatism, to model a personal empowerment program around a credential when a major criticism of school and society is based on disavowing credentialing?

It is also clear that traditional institutions feel they own the high school credential. In practice, if one cannot deny financial resources to these empowerment programs, the next line of defense is to deny the use of the credential; traditional educational systems are using this strategy in resisting the empowerment programs. If one refuses to seek public funds or to partake of the credit system, it appears that empowerment programs would not be readily replicable and possibly could survive only on resources and students attracted by a charismatic leader.

An example of this contradiction can be seen in the struggle of the Alternative School Network in the Chicago area to gain access to public funding. A political conflict of several years standing between the public agencies for adult education and the Network resulted in the promise in 1982 to provide public funding for the latter. Alternative adult schools within the Network have, in part, gained access to the high school credential through some sympathetic schools in Catholic dioceses. However, a counterthrust is now in progress to challenge the legality of parochial schools' "loan" of the high school diploma to adult empowerment programs.

Educators in credit-bearing programs have their own set of contradictions which apparently pit philosophy against practice. One such problem stems from marginality and the suspicion traditional educators have for nontraditional practice. For example, these adult educators must bear the burden of the charlatan charge. The cheap degree from the mail order university makes good copy. The cheap degree from the traditional educational institution, no less (and potentially more) destructive because it is legitimated by traditional methods, is very hard to document but no less a reality. Yet the former is condemned while the latter is condoned. Accordingly, nontraditional credit bearing programs are continually forced to defend their philosophy of openness and alternatives because of the bad practice of others not due to a direct relationship to their programs. To relieve this pressure, nontraditional program leaders become more conventional than the traditional leaders — in direct contradiction to their own philosophy.

Methodological Issues. Contradictions between philosophy and practice can be seen within credit-bearing alternatives based on methodology. These contradictions occur when the educator attempts to translate experiential learning into credit. Actually experiential learning has always been a part of traditional education. As Houle (1977) argues, earliest formalized education was based on an experiential model. In higher education there has always been laboratory and internship options to give students opportunities for experiential learning. This type of experiential learning is now designated as collegiate sponsored to distinguish it from the nontraditional proponents who give credit for prior experiential learning gained through life experiences or by nonformal means. Traditional educators resist, if not actively oppose, the concept of crediting prior learning. Traditional educators contradict themselves in the extraordinary rigor in judging prior experiential learning even though ordinary standards suffice when this same kind of learning is sponsored by the institution. Actually, traditional educators typically go to great lengths — usually in the name of academic freedom — to allow subjective judgments and permit considerable latitude for faculty in assessing traditional classroom or sponsored experiential learning. It therefore seems that the problem is not that the learning is experiential but rather than the experiential learning was done without prior ratification or through formal enrollment at an educational institution.

Since collegiate-sponsored learning as well as prior-experiential learning is not supervised by the faculty but by an employee within the institution at which the student is assigned, it would seem that some other explanation of faculty resistance must be found. One explanation is that allowing credit for learning outside the institution creates faculty opposition because it results in the loss of credit hours rather than because of philosophical differences about who should evaluate learning and when and where learning should occur.

The issues of translating experiential learning into credit and eventually into a credential have imposed curious practices on humanistic educators involved in credit-bearing nontraditional programs. Such educators value the autonomy of the learner not only for behavior which can be regarded as learning but also for those imaginative areas of learning which do not lend themselves to measurement. However, because of campus politics and practice, educators can unknowingly disregard a valued part of learning simply because it cannot be reduced to measurement. Therefore, one may see humanists practicing as behaviorists casting nontraditional credit bearing programs in terms of competency- or performance-based models. The result is that nontraditional programs are reduced to the most limited of traditional practices.

Another methodological issue which contradicts the philosophy of credit-bearing alternatives concerns the inconsistency that results when curricular practices resulting from one set of assumptions about adult learners and learning are met with a contradictory set of assumptions espoused by the traditional systems. To what extent can learners be in charge of goal setting, methodological choice, and evaluation when traditional institutions maintain ultimate control of these functions? Thus Malcolm Knowles (1975) writes of "self-directed learning," in which the learner negotiates the ends and means of learning with the "facilitator." One can argue that this kind of practice will be appropriated by the educational agent and that the learner will have only an illusion of power. After all, the external rewards the learner seeks actually reside in the institution.

In summary, all three types of nontraditional continuing education present profound problems when the alternative systems are converted to practice. The financing of programs becomes a basic issue for free form and personal empowerment models and a concern for credit bearing alternative models. Credentialing issues can be observed both in personal empowerment and in credit bearing programs, since credentials can be used as a political instrument to deny growth or survival. New methods to obtain credentials are continually challenged in credit bearing programs by traditional schools though these schools avoid similar critical assessment of their own methods. Methodological issues in credit bearing alternatives were identified as points of conflict between philosophy and practice. Prior experiential learning outside of institutional sponsorship faces strong oppositon. Learners may be placed in charge of their own learning in theory but not in actuality. These areas of conflict within the three types of nontraditional education are one set of problems and there are other similar sets of problems.

Conflicts in Practice Among Types of Nontraditional Education

Where the Battle Is Fought. Conflict arises between those in credit bearing programs and those who are disenchanted with traditional institutions. A criticism leveled by the latter is that educators working within credit systems either do not understand the problem, are well-meaning liberal thinkers with misplaced optimism regarding the ability of institutions to change, or have so much vested interest in the institution that they avoid doing what they know they must in order to force educational institutions to make qualitative changes.

Further, both the free form and personal empowerment adult educators are suspicious about the motivation behind traditional institutional sponsorship of nontraditional programs. The suspicion is that the institution is not responding to legitimate student requirements, but rather is responding to survival needs — given the demographic trends which produce fewer enrollments of younger students. In so doing, the argument goes, the ultimate goal has not changed, for credits (and credentialing) will be extended to this new clientele thereby increasing continued legitimization by institutions.

Appropriate Practice. Free form educators, if they were interested in so doing, could challenge the personal empowerment educators about assumptions concerning the learner and the desired ends of education. While both kinds of nontraditional educators agree that the central philosophical issue is the freedom of the individual to have equal access to and control of his or her own learning, the two differ about implementing that philosophy.

Free form educators believe that people are natural learners and that it is innate to direct one's own learning. Tough and his followers suggest that less than 2 percent of all personal learning projects are for credit. The role of the educator then is probably moving toward one in which status is obliterated (everyone a teacher; everyone a learner), and all individuals should be assisted in learning how to learn. To the extent that schooling has blunted their curiosity or stifled their potential for becoming autonomous learners, adults need educators who provide the environment for assisting the learner to discover the joy of self-directed learning and in so doing to reach the fullest possible personal potential. Such learners would then be capable of understanding and making decisions about the complex problems faced in high technology societies, and be able to help create more responsible societies.

Personal empowerment educators, on the other hand, see the basic issue as a power relationship between the oppressed and the oppressor. While they might agree that all individuals are oppressed to a degree by society's structures, they would contend that some are clearly more oppressed by reason of their being denied an equitable share of society's resources and opportunities. Further, the elites of society (who may be ideal, self-directed learners seeking their human potential), having had more resources and opportunities, continue to increase their advantage by taking further resources and opportunities from the underclass. This is not done openly but by institutions developed and controlled by those who have experienced society's largess. Thus one observes social class differences between the students in free form versus personal empowerment programs.

Empowerment advocates view education as never neutral; it is either liberating or oppressing. Traditional schooling oppresses since it is responsible for domesticating learners by teaching them that they are responsible for their condition or as one writer expresses it, "blaming the victim" (Ryan, 1971). Thus goes the thesis, and two potential conflicts in practice appear. Free form educators would probably be disturbed by the fact that, in practice, empowerment educators (facilitators) assume a philosophical view of liberatory education that may well not be shared with the learner. To the extent that the liberatory curriculum is defined by the facilitators' values, is the learner in control? Further, could not education based on these values result in mere propagandizing for a political end? On the other hand, empowerment educators must feel uneasy about the free form educators' stress on individual autonomy, which appears to work best for the educated elites who have less need for collective political action. In fact, some critics would argue that individualism as a central value in our society is antithetical to bringing about an equitable society. Individualism as a way of life may be most prized by those who do not deal daily with survival issues.

Pragmatism. The credit bearing educators take issue, if not directly then indirectly, with free form educators in at least two ways. First, most believe that a rational sorting mechanism, like an educational institution, has to exist in order to match individuals with personnel needs in a highly functional mass society. Furthermore, if one did believe that such a world were possible where order and efficiency could be achieved without imposed structures, the fact is that credit and credentials are so basic to the organization of society (although imperfect mechanisms) that it is either impossible to eliminate them without destroying the system or not worth the confusion that such an effort would engender.

With this same practical argument, credit-bearing educators take issue with personal empowerment proponents. When accused of a lack of risk taking in carrying out their philosophy (remaining within the institution), credit-bearing nontraditionalists respond with similar *ad hominem* rebukes. The accusation is that the radical rhetoric of personal empowerment educators goes far beyond their practical ideals because the context of the problem is qualitatively distinct in postindustrial societies. Thus the potential for deschooling societies may be appropriate for Third World countries but not for postindustrial societies which base their existence on requiring thirteen to twenty or more years of schooling for all citizens. In the latter case empowerment programs tend to be reformist, at best, rather than radical or revolutionary practices.

In summary, conflicts among the three types of nontraditional continuing educators center on problems of consistency in practice and philosophy. There is conflict among educators as to whether the best place to counteract the dysfunction of traditional education is within or without the institution. Part of the conflict is based on the notion that the vested interest of the educators, rather than their philosophy, determines the place of operation. Another part of the conflict arises from the suspicion that institutions cannot be qualitatively changed because means have become ends.

Clearly, human potential programs based on a philosophy emphasizing the autonomy of the learner are in conflict with empowerment programs whose goals are based on altering social arrangements, even though the anti-institutional analyses on which both these practices are based appear similar.

Finally, pragmatic differences result in conflicts in terms of the contention that schools or credits are not necessary in large postindustrial societies.

Conclusions

In discussing the conflicts between philosophy and practice within and among the three types of nontraditional continuing educators, the starting point is that philosophical systems are symbolic abstractions of relationships which are idealistically constructed on selected assumptions. Only philosophers can be purists. When philosophy systematically and consciously informs their practice, practitioners do not operate in a world which conforms to their assumptions. They compete with alternative philosophies and alternative practices. In the area of practice, the educator must negotiate philosophy. Choices are made as to what can be deleted or altered with the least damage to the intended outcomes. It is not problematic that inconsistencies occur when a thoughtfully conceived system of values is put into practice. What is worrisome is that continuing educators develop and operate programs without a clearly visualized set of values in which the adult learner and societal well-being are central concerns.

All nontraditional continuing educators who have reflected on their assumptions about the adult learner and adult education share something important; they are critically conscious of their value system. They have more to gain from cooperative action than from divisiveness that arises from conflict within and among various programs. At a time when much adult education gets subsumed into the schooling mode — as a result of conservatism, convenience, changing societal needs, or institutional and professional self-interest — it will take the combined energy of all socially and critically self-conscious continuing educators to create, preserve and strengthen sound alternatives to the bureaucratization of continuing education.

References

Adams, F. *Unearthing Seeds of Fire.* Winston-Salem: John F. Blair, 1975.

Commission on Nontraditional Study. *Diversity by Design.* San Francisco: Jossey-Bass, 1973.

Draves, W. *The Free University.* Chicago: Follett-Association Press, 1980.

Freire, P. *Pedagogy of the Oppressed.* New York: Herder and Herder, 1970.

Gross, R. and Dimenderg, E. *Meeting the Needs of Independent Scholars.* New York: College Board, 1980.

Heaney, T. "Adult Learning and Empowerment: Toward a Theory of Liberatory Education." Unpublished doctoral dissertation, Union Graduate School, 1980.

Houle, C. O. "Deep Traditions of Experiential Learning." In M. T. Keeton, (Ed.) *Experiential Learning.* San Francisco: Jossey-Bass, 1977.

Knowles, M. *Self-Directed Learning.* Chicago: Association Press/Follett, 1975.

Ryan, W. *Blaming the Victim.* New York: Pantheon Books, 1971.

Simpson, E. L. "Some Dimensions of Nontraditional." *Thresholds in Education,* 1977, *3* (3), 2-3.

Toffler, A. *Future Shock.* New York: Bantam Books, 1970.

Tough, A. *The Adult's Learning Projects.* Toronto: The Ontario Institute for Studies in Education, 1971.

Phyllis M. Cunningham is associate professor and chair of adult continuing education at Northern Illinois University. Experience as dean of the Center for Open Learning in the City Colleges of Chicago and a board member of Instituto del Progresso Latino, a community based personal empowerment program, serves as basis for her observations in this article.

Philosophy and practice are interactive in continuing education.
Practitioners can take several approaches in strengthening this bond.

Some Thoughts on the Relationship Between Theory and Practice

Sharan B. Merriam

The purpose of this sourcebook is to explore the relationship between philosophy and practice. An underlying assumption of the editor and authors of this sourcebook is that the two should be united even more closely if continuing education is to become a mature field of study and practice. Practitioners can benefit from the experiences and theorizing of those who have gone before. Philosophy thus informs practice; it can guide administrators, teachers, and counselors in their everyday planning and decision making. In order to advance, however, the field needs to do more than pass down accumulated wisdom to novice practitioners. Practice must also test past theory and contribute to the building of new theory. This is, of course, easier said than done in a field such a continuing education that is characterized by pragmatic concerns, a multidisciplinary foundation, and a marketplace orientation.

The seven case examples presented in this sourcebook provide a data base for assessing the extent to which philosophy and practice are interactive in continuing education. The tension-bearing relationship between philosophy and practice, Elias points out in the first chapter, can be described as directive, explanatory, critical, and imaginative. Whether evaluating adult basic education (ABE) teachers, developing a continuing education program at a small col-

S. Merriam (Ed.). *New Directions for Continuing Education: Linking Philosophy and Practice*, no. 15.
San Francisco: Jossey-Bass, September 1982.

lege, or assessing needs in an African village, these elements of the philosophy-practice dialectic can be found in varying degrees.

Explanation and Direction

Theory helps to explain the ends and objectives of practice. The nature of the continuing education program for adults at Clarke College in Iowa, for example, reflects the philosophy of the director. Making classes accessible to adults and providing the support services needed to facilitate their returning to college reflect the director's commitment to, above all else, the adult person's needs in a higher education setting. Conflicts with those who hold other views of the College's goals were inevitable during the development of the program.

Closely aligned to explanation is the idea that theory can direct practice. Evaluating adult basic education teachers is an excellent example of working from a sound theoretical base. Jones and Lowe write that evaluation as judgment is incongruous with what we know about adults as learners. If we agree with the assumptions underlying an andragogical approach to adult learning, and if we treat ABE teachers as they are expected to deal with students, then improving teacher performance becomes the goal of evaluation not a judgment. The authors offer some practical means of evaluating teachers from an andragogical framework which they have found to be successful in practice. Other examples of theory directing practice are discussed in Flanigan and Smith's analysis of decision making in a large urban continuing education program. In program planning, evaluation, and the hiring of instructors, continuing education theory guides action.

Criticism and Imagination

Of the four characteristics of the theory/practice relationship, the notion of criticism best highlights the interaction between reflection and action. A theory provides the rationale for organizing activities in certain ways. In a sense, theory also challenges us to think about the way we do things. Donald Campbell (this volume) observes that the impact of mandatory continuing education (MCE) has been felt in the way in which medical educators go about planning programs. Partially due to the pressure of providing programs under a mandatory edict, and partially due to familiarity, one and only one model of program planning is typically followed. This model offers a rationale for planning programs in the most expedient manner possible, and the realities of MCE have reinforced the use of this particular procedure. While the model has its advantages, it tends, in Campbell's words, to treat "educational planning as a series of steps to be accomplished, rather than a more holistic process."

Practice also offers a testing ground for theory. Observing how theory works in the real world causes theory to be rejected in some cases, modified or reformulated in other cases. Merrill Ewert (this volume) suggests that the theory behind participatory planning needs some sort of refinement in order to accommodate problems encountered in practice. When participants were actually included in the identification of needs and the planning of programs in African villages, the following problems evolved: participants, in articulating their perceived needs, expected the facilitator to produce an immediate solution; in discovering that the cause of their problems lay with the political structure, another group of villagers was dissuaded from action that would have been suicidal; the credibility of the teacher comes into question when adults are unacquainted with participatory methods; and programs developed by participants may pose a threat to the established order.

That the theory/practice relationship can be imaginative is illustrated in the chapter on nontraditional continuing education. The philosophical assumptions underlying three forms of nontraditional continuing education — credit bearing, free form, and empowerment models — essentially reject traditional (especially institutional) educational practice. As these forms become tested in a world where credentials, finances, and politics are unavoidable realities, imaginative variations are likely to evolve. In nontraditional education, we have a case of theory rejecting present practice and offering creative alternatives. Practice of these new forms will no doubt result in modification of theory.

What Practitioners Can Do

The case examples in this sourcebook give us some sense of the interaction of philosophy and practice. This interaction can be explanatory, directive, critical, or imaginative. What comes through even more clearly, however, is that those who practice continuing education are under enormous pressure to do that which is most expedient. Pressure comes from many sources: There is never enough financial support, space, or staff; the parent institution often has goals incongruent or different from those of the continuing education program; the community must be served as well as individual learners; and evaluation and accountability issues must be addressed. The practitioner finds him- or herself shifting priorities, juggling values, and skirting issues in order to maintain a program. If any philosophical orientation guides the practice of continuing education, it is that of pragmatism — doing what is the most practical, what will accomplish desired results in as expedient a manner as possible. Flanagan and Smith and Koeper's chapters are good illustrations of how practitioners operate under pressure. Typically, several values or criteria are taken into account in dealing with a situation. That priority among many which is temporarily assigned the greatest weight is the one that responds to the element in the situation exerting the most pressure. This priority becomes, in Flanagan and Smith's terms, the bottom line. Policy is then organized around the bottom line. Hopefully, the policy will not preempt subsequent priorities. In any case, the actual practice of continuing education relies heavily upon comparison of anticipated outcomes and upon past experiences, rather than theory.

What, then, is the role of philosophy in the practice of continuing education, and how can philosophical concepts be more useful to administrators, counselors, and teachers in the future? Once again we can turn to the case examples for answers. In some instances, a philosophical framework does guide practice. The evaluation of ABE teachers is one good example, as is the development of a continuing education division at a small liberal arts college in Iowa. Other situations, decision making with regard to the allocation of scarce resources, for example, highlight the need for theory. In still other situations, theory needs to be modified, expanded, or adjusted to resolve incongruities as it is put into practice. Aspects of nontraditional education, for example, are inconsistent with the underlying philosophical assumptions. Likewise, the theory behind participatory planning has yet to offer guidance in dealing with the crucial issues arising out of implementation.

The question becomes one of what practitioners can do to strengthen the bond between theory and practice. Whenever possible, theory should be brought to bear in situations that require goal setting, decision making, and value clarification. Educators can also experiment in their practice, actively reflect upon the process of education, and evaluate the ends of that process. In so doing, contributions can be made to the theory of continuing education. Don Campbell points out that even in a mandatory continuing medical education environment, practitioners can see opportunities to introduce alternative program planning models that are more in line with the field's views on adult learning. Finally, Elias, in Chapter One, suggests that the theory-practice split in continuing education can be addressed through integrating activities in the training of adult and continuing educators in graduate school, and in making more of an effort to unite the two at conferences and in our professional publications.

Practical Nature of Theory and Philosophy

In addition to strengthening the bond between philosophy and practice, attention to assumptions and underlying values can be of practical help to continuing educators, in that attention to philosophy can strengthen decisions, professionalism, instruction, and communication.

Philosophy provides guidelines for policy decisions. The everyday tasks of setting policy and making decisions can be facilitated if one is aware of his or her underlying values. A public school continuing education director, for example, need not agonize over whether to apply for federal ABE money if his or her philosophical priorities are clearly established. Likewise, one's philosophical orientation can be useful in deciding whether some form of certification (diploma, continuing education units, credit) must necessarily accompany a learning activity.

Philosophy contributes to professionalism. Having a philosophic orientation separates the professional continuing educator from the paraprofessional in that professionals are aware of what they are doing and why they are doing it. A philosophy offers goals, values, and attitudes to strive for. It thus can be motivating, inspiring, and energizing to the practitioner. The professional has an end in mind, as well as the means, a vision which makes sense out of the means. Suttle (1982) addresses this point in a recent issue of *Adult Education*. The difference between having a philosophy and not having one, he says, "is ultimately the difference between merely having an assortment of so-called facts at one's disposal and being able to understand what one allegedly knows." The extent to which continuing educators can be viewed as professional will enhance their standing with other educators and legitimize their role in the community.

Philosophy directly affects curriculum and instruction. One's view of the adult learner, the learning process, and the goals of adult education guides the selection of content and planning of instruction. If, for example, one believes that adults learn best when directing their own learning, then opportunities to do this must be incorporated into a learning situation. The educator who believes that people learn best when the content or material is arranged in certain ways will select curricula and plan instruction differently from those who place the student, rather than the subject, at the center of a learning activity.

Philosophy facilitates good interpersonal communication. Continuing educators who know what they believe and how their beliefs impact upon practice can bring clarity and understanding to interaction with others, especially over issues of mutual concern. For example, upon discovering his philosophical roots in progressivism, a community school director remarked that now he could finally understand why he and a certain corporate training director were always at odds with each other during advisory panel meetings.

The above four areas represent concrete ways in which philosophy can be of help to continuing educators. More subtle, and probably more important, is the indirect impact practitioners who develop and use a philosophical orientation can have upon the field of continuing education. Informed practitioners do what the authors of this sourcebook have done: they observe what they are doing, ask why they are doing it, and look for opportunities to further enhance their practice. Inconsistencies may occur when philosophy is put into practice, and a lack of theory may be discovered when one looks for guidelines to action. These are the by-products of making a conscious effort to unite theory and practice in continuing education. Such efforts can only lead to the development of better theory, which in turn will lead to more informed practice.

References

Suttle, B. "Adult Education: No Need for Theories?" *Adult Education,* 1982, *32* (2), 104–107.

Sharan B. Merriam is associate professor of adult continuing education at Northern Illinois University. She is coauthor of Philosophical Foundations of Adult Education *and* Adult Education: Foundations of Practice.

References are provided in four areas: characteristics of philosophy, philosophy and education, individual philosophies, and education.

Sources in Philosophy and Continuing Education

Jerold W. Apps

This chapter provides annotated references in four broad areas: the characteristics of philosophy, philosophy and education, some philosophers and their philosophies, and continuing education and philosophy.

The Characteristics of Philosophy

For those who are interested in exploring the application of philosophy to continuing education but who are somewhat uncomfortable with the language and writings in philosophy, the following references may be helpful.

Lacey, A. R. *A Dictionary of Philosophy*. London: Routledge & Kegan Paul, 1976.
In a succinct, albeit sometimes too brief fashion, Lacey discusses such terms as free will and determinism, good, ethics, and, of course, the various philosophies such as existentialism, essentialism, and pragmatism. Many noted philosophers are also mentioned, and their works are very briefly described.

Ortega y Gasset, J. *What Is Philosophy?* New York: W. W. Norton, 1960.
Gasset, a prominent European philosopher, explains the diffences between science and philosophy. He explains that the "philosopher is not inter-

S. Merriam (Ed.). *New Directions for Continuing Education: Linking Philosophy and Practice,* no. 15. San Francisco: Jossey-Bass, September 1982.

93

ested in each thing that exists, in its separate end, one might say, its private existence, but in the aggregate of all there is; consequently, in everything which makes up that aggregate, and consequently in that aspect of each thing insofar as it concerns the others, its place, role, and nature in the entirety of things—the public life of each thing, so to speak, what it is worth, what it represents in the sovereign scope of universal existence" (p. 76). By "thing" Gasset means physical and living things as well as abstract ideas.

In addition to talking about the place of philosophy, he describes how one goes about thinking philosophically as contrasted with how one thinks scientifically.

Pirsig, R. M. *Zen and the Art of Motorcycle Maintenance.* New York: William Morrow, 1974.

Though written as a novel, this book explores the contributions philosophical thinking can make, particularly in the area of value exploration. Pirsig discusses differences between scientific and philosophical inquiry, and writes, "Traditional scientific method. . . [is] good for seeing where you've been. It's good for testing the truth of what you think you know, but it can't tell you where you ought to go, unless where you ought to go is a continuation of where you were going in the past. Creativity, originality, inventiveness, intuition, imagination—'unstuckness,' in other words—are completely outside its domain" (p. 80).

Russell, B. *The Art of Philosophizing and Other Essays.* New York: Philosophical Library, 1968.

Russell, B. *A History of Western Philosophy.* New York: Simon and Schuster, 1945.

In *The Art of Philosophizing,* Russell tells us what philosophy is and how we go about doing it. He writes that "philosophy tells us how to proceed when we want to find out what may be true, or is *most likely* to be true, where it is impossible to know with certainty what *is* true."

In *A History of Western Philosophy,* Russell begins with the presocratic philosophers and brings us up to the present time. As he discusses each philosophy he places it in a particular historical perspective. For those wanting a broad view of Western philosophy, written in a highly readable manner, start with this book.

Problems and Philosophy

For a brief introduction to some of the problems with which philosophy deals and how it deals with them, the following references will be useful.

Adler, M. J. *Aristotle for Everybody: Difficult Thought Made Easy.* New York: Macmillan, 1978.

Adler, M. J. *Six Great Ideas.* New York: Macmillan, 1981.

In *Aristotle* Adler discusses three major directions for human activity: the human as maker, as doer, and as knower. In *Six Great Ideas,* Adler examines the ideas by which we judge: truth, goodness, and beauty; and the three ideas we act on: liberty, equality, and justice. Adler's work avoids the "in" jargon of philosophy and discusses philosophical concepts in a way the person untrained in philosophy can understand.

Durant, W. *The Pleasures of Philosophy.* New York: Simon and Schuster, 1929; 1953.

Durant takes the practical problems humans face and examines them from a philosophical perspective. He explores such questions as What is truth? Is man a machine? What is beauty? and Is progress a delusion? He also deals with the problems of our changing morals; the modern woman; the mortality of nations; the difficulties of freedom; and the making of religion.

Matson, F. W. *The Idea of Man.* New York: Delacorte Press, 1976.

For those interested in exploring the basic foundations of human beings as learners, here is an interesting and thought-provoking discussion.

Matson discusses the new humanism, the idea of human beings as creators rather than as determined creatures or persons entirely influenced by their environments. He traces various ideas about the nature of human beings, discussing humans as Freud, Darwin, and others saw them.

Royce, J. R. *The Encapsulated Man.* New York: D. Van Nostrand, 1964.

Royce discusses the importance of philosophical thought. He writes: "This book represents one encapsulated man's views as to why 'specialization' is a profoundly serious problem in today's world, why we must remove some cobwebs in our thinking on this matter and at least seriously entertain the idea of developing 'generalists' as well as 'specialists'" (p. v). More than half of the book focuses on how human beings search for meaning in their lives.

Philosophy and Education

The following resources show how philosophy and the broad field of education relate, including how philosophy looks at some of the questions education faces.

Buford, T. O. *Toward a Philosophy of Education.* New York: Holt, Rinehart and Winston, 1969.

Buford helps us understand particular problems in education from the perspective of the educational philosophies: perennialism, progressivism, reconstructionism, essentialism, and existentialism. For each philosophy he includes writings from people who subscribe to that philosophy. For those who have problems with philosophical jargon, Buford includes a glossary at the end of his book.

Cahn, S. J. *The Philosophical Foundations of Education.* New York: Harper & Row, 1970.

For someone who wants a broad sampling of the writings of traditional and modern day philosophers as applied to education, here is a starting place. Cahn has selections from Plato, Aristotle, Locke, Rousseau, Kant, as well as Dewey, Whitehead, Russell, Maritain, and Hook. The last section of the book includes a series of articles on analytic philosophy and education.

Henry, N. B. (Ed.). *Modern Philosophies and Education.* Chicago, Ill.: University of Chicago Press, 1955.

This, the fifty-fourth yearbook of the National Society for the Study of Education, includes articles on philosophizing about education, a realistic view of education and human society, an experimentalist approach to education, a Marxist philosophy of education, and a linguistic approach to problems of education. The book is written for those not accustomed to reading philosophical writing.

Johnson, J. A. and others. *Introduction to the Foundations of American Education.* Boston: Allyn & Bacon, 1969.

Johnson defines philosophy and then introduces metaphysics, epistemology, and axiology with a brief explanation of each. He explains briefly the classical philosophies of idealism, realism, neo-Thomism, experimentalism, and existentialism. Finally, he introduces the educational philosophies: essentialism, perennialism, progressivism, reconstructionism, and existentialism. The book is easy to read, and contains basic information on the subject.

Marshall, J. P. *The Teacher and His Philosophy.* Lincoln, Neb.: Professional Educators Publications, 1973.

Marshall discusses why educational philosophy is important and the kinds of benefits the educator can derive from developing his or her own educational philosophy. He then discusses idealism, realism, perennialism, pragmatism, and existentialism.

Smith, P. G. (Ed.). *Theories of Value and Problems of Education.* Urbana: University of Illinois Press, 1970.

The field of continuing education has begun to recognize the problems of ethics and ethical decision making for teachers and administrators of continuing education programs. This book helps the practitioner by looking at ethical questions, including essays on the following topics: Does ethics make a difference?; education and morals; teaching and telling; and educational values and goals. Contributors include Harry Broudy, Jean Piaget, and Israel Scheffler.

Some Philosophers and Their Philosophies

Adult and continuing education has been influenced by several philosophers, a few of whom are included below.

Dewey, J. *Democracy and Education.* New York: Macmillan, 1964
Dewey, J. *Experience and Education.* New York: Collier, 1938; 1963.
Dewey, J. *How We Think.* Chicago: Henry Regnery, 1933.
Boydston, J. A. (Ed.). *Guide to the Works of John Dewey.* Carbondale: Southern
   Illinois University Press, 1970.

   Viewed by many as the father of present day educational philosophy,
Dewey contributed greatly to the examination of fundamental questions in
education. Dewey's educational philosophy, called progressivism, is based on
a problem-solving approach to learning. In *How We Think,* Dewey described
his problem-solving approach. *Democracy and Education* helps us see how Dewey
examined the problems of education in a democratic society, and *Experience and
Education* gives us a glimpse of how Dewey saw the importance of experience in
learning.

   Boydston has brought together articles about Dewey's philosophy and
philosophic method; his logic and theory of knowledge; his ethics, his social,
political, and legal philosophy; his theory of art; his theory of valuation; his
philosophy of religion; his social and political commentary; and his views on
education and schooling.

Freire, P. *Education for Critical Consciousness.* New York: Seabury, 1967.
Freire, P. *Pedagogy of the Oppressed.* New York: Herder and Herder, 1970.
Grabowski, S. M. (Ed.). *Paulo Freire: A Revolutionary Dilemma for the Adult
   Educator.* Syracuse, N.Y.: Syracuse University Publications in Continuing
   Education, 1972.

   A philosopher and an adult educator, Freire examines and challenges
present approaches to education, especially adult literacy education. He
challenges what he calls "banking education," the depositing of knowledge in
the heads of learners. Freire calls for reform in adult education, particularly
for a reshaping of the relationship between teacher and student, and the relationship of students to each other. The Grabowski anthology examines Freire's
ideas about continuing education from several perspectives, some favoring
and some opposed.

Goble, F. G. *The Third Force.* New York: Grossman, 1970.

   In recent years, many continuing educators have subscribed to a humanistic philosophy of continuing education. Goble discusses the historical
perspective of this movement and focuses particularly on the contributions of
Abraham Maslow to humanistic psychology.

Illich, I. *Deschooling Society.* New York: Harper and Row, 1970; 1971.

   Illich is an example of a radical adult educator; he argues for abolishing
formal schools and establishing in their place learning networks. Though often
controversial and discounted as antiestablishment, Illich raises important philosophical questions for the adult educator—particularly questions about the
role formal institutions play in education.

Tillich, P. *The Courage To Be.* New Haven, Conn.: Yale University Press, 1952.

Tillich, an existentialist, writes about the meaning of courage in the history of Western thought. He discusses being, nonbeing, and anxiety; courage and participation; courage and individualization; and the existentialist forms of the courage required to be as oneself.

In his discussion of courage and participation, Tillich writes: "Self and world are correlated, and so are individualization and participation. For this is what participation means: being a part of something from which one is, at the same time, separated. . . . A part of a whole is not identical with the whole to which it belongs. But the whole is what it is only with the part" (p. 88).

For those interested in existentialist thought as applied to present day problems and concerns, Tillich is one starting place.

Whitehead, A. N. *The Aims of Education.* New York: Macmillan, 1929.

Along with Dewey, Whitehead was a powerful contributor to educational philosophy. His ideas, radical in their day, continue to be radical today. For instance, he thought that dividing universities into departments and segmenting knowledge into courses was the bane of an education. He argued for the interdependence of disciplines. As the title suggests, Whitehead spends most of his time in this book talking about what education can hope to accomplish.

Philosophy and Continuing Education

Writings about philosophy and continuing have begun to increase in recent years. These writings have taken at least three directions. Some authors have looked broadly at philosophy and continuing education, attempting to show connections and to explain the philosophic roots of continuing education. Others have chosen to write a philosophy of continuing education from their perspective, and still others have focused on approaches to doing philosophy.

Apps, J. W. *Problems in Continuing Education.* New York: McGraw-Hill, 1979.

Apps, J. W. *Toward a Working Philosophy of Adult Education.* Syracuse, N.Y.: Syracuse University Publications in Continuing Education, 1973.

Apps, J. W. "A Foundation for Action." In C. Klevens (Ed.), *Materials and Methods in Continuing Education.* Los Angeles: Klevens, 1976.

In "A Foundation for Action," Apps presents a belief analysis process consisting of four phases:

1. Identifying beliefs held about adult education: beliefs about the adult learner, about the purposes for adult education agencies and institutions, about the teaching and learning process for adults, and about the role of the adult educator.

2. Searching for contradictions among beliefs held.

3. Discovering bases for beliefs. These bases include sources of beliefs and evidence that supports beliefs.

4. Making judgments about bases for the particular beliefs held.

Apps is concerned with adult educators' learning how to do philosophy, particularly developing their own working philosophies. In *Toward a Working Philosophy of Adult Education,* he suggests a framework for developing a personal philosophy consisting of: (1) beliefs about the adult learner, (2) beliefs about the purpose of adult education, (3) beliefs about content, and (4) beliefs about the teaching-learning process.

In *Problems in Continuing Education,* Apps expands on this basic framework by suggesting questions to be raised within each of the framework areas. In many instances, he also presents alternative answers for the continuing educator to consider. In the final two chapters of the problems book, Apps analyzes research in continuing education from a philosophical perspective.

Bergevin, P. *A Philosophy of Adult Education.* New York: Seabury Press, 1967.

Bergevin, an adult educator, has developed a statement of his adult education philosophy. It includes such topics as the meanings of the term "adult education," major problems in the education of adults, and concepts to implement the education of adults.

Buford, T. O. *Philosophy for Adults.* Washington, D.C.: University Press of America, 1980.

Buford's premise is that "every adult is a philosopher. In the changing patterns and stages of their lives, adults face problems which drive them to examine again and again those beliefs and values which form the basis of their life styles (p. xiii). *Philosophy for Adults* uses the case method to help readers examine and evaluate the assumptions that underlie many lifelike situations associated with various developmental tasks common to adulthood. The essays that follow each case suggest possible solutions, but the readers are not guided toward any preconceived final answers to the problems. Instead, readers are led to see how philosophy can be used as a valuable resource to guide adults through crises and periods of transition.

Elias, J. L., and Merriam, S. *Philosophical Foundations of Adult Education.* Huntington, N.Y.: Krieger, 1980.

Six philosophies of adult education are the focus of Elias and Merriam's work. The authors discuss liberal adult education, progressive adult education, behaviorist adult education, humanistic adult education, radical adult education, and an analytic philosophy of adult education. For each of these philosophies, the authors present the roots, the persons identified with the philosophy, and some of the approaches. For instance, within what they call radical adult education philosophy, they mention such persons as Theodore Brameld, Jonathan Kozol, John Holt, Paul Goodman, Ivan Illich, and Paulo Freire.

Approaches include Freedom Schools in the South during the 1960s and Freire's radical approach to literacy education.

Within the Behaviorist philosophy they include Thorndike, Pavlov, Watson, and B. F. Skinner. Approaches used in adult education, which have been influenced by the behaviorist philosophy, are programmed learning, behavioral objectives, and competency-based teacher education.

The book demonstrates how the various philosophies have benefited from one another and how an understanding of these philosophies can help adult educators to clarify their own philosophy of education.

Lawson, K. H. *Philosophical Concepts and Values in Adult Education.* Nottingham, England: Barnes and Humby, Ltd., 1975.

Lawson, using the approach of the analytic philosopher, examines several key ideas within adult education: definition of adult education, learning situations, student-centered programs, personal development, and political adult education. He explains the meaning of the concepts, discusses the nature of justifications, and points out problems that language presents.

He also draws conclusions, one of which questions the adult education approach in which the adult educator takes a passive role. He believes it important that the adult educator be the one who helps to lead the learner from the known to the unknown.

Aside from his conclusions, which often run counter to much humanistic adult education espoused in this country, his work is a fine example of how to do philosophical analysis.

Lindeman, E. C. *The Meaning of Adult Education.* Montreal: Harvest House, 1926; 1961.

Lindeman writes a clear statement of philosophy for adult education, and though prepared in 1926, the statement has as much relevance now as it had then. Lindeman's writing is both an example of the issues that concern a philosopher, as well as the approach a philosopher uses in writing about issues. Lindeman was a social philosopher, one who cared about human beings and their welfare and who saw adult education as one approach toward social change.

Some of the topics he developed in this classic piece of adult-education writing were an examination of self-expression and creativity, an analysis of power and freedom, and the need for all of us to appreciate. He also wrote eloquently about the problems our society faces with specialism: "In the modern world of specialism only a small sector of personality is set into motion through vocational activities. We all tend to become specialists — which means that we all tend to become fractional personalities" (p. 34).

In his discussion of freedom he wrote: "Those individuals are free who know their powers and capacities as well as their limitations; who seek a way of life which utilizes their total personalities; who aim to alter their conduct in relation to a changing environment in which they are conscious of being active agents. Each of these components of freedom is dependent upon a degree of intelligence and is realizable in terms of education" (p. 50).

McKenzie, L. *Adult Education and the Burden of the Future.* Washington, D.C.: University Press of America, 1978.

After saying something about what philosophy is and the relation of adult education to philosophy, McKenzie devotes most of this work to his views on adult education philosophy. It is a good example of how to think and write philosophically, and it provides a reasonable statement of one adult educator's philosophy. Another unique contribution McKenzie makes is the tying of adult education to the philosophy of history.

Paterson, R. W. K. *Values, Education, and the Adult.* London, England: Routledge & Kegan Paul, 1979.

Paterson, following a philosophical analysis approach, examines such continuing education concepts as definition of adult education, educational objectives, education processes, and the relationship of adult education to society. He takes some rather controversial positions, at least for many adult educators in this country. Paterson refuses to see adult education as contributing to practical or social purposes, thus taking a rather narrow view of the field of vocational education. He writes: "Vocational courses aim, not at the development of persons as persons, but at the preparation of functionaries." According to Paterson, adult education is not adult education unless it focuses on liberal studies.

Jerald W. Apps is professor of adult education and chairman of the Department of Continuing and Vocational Education at the University of Wisconsin, Madison. He is the author of numerous books and articles in adult continuing education.

Index